YOUNG PEOPLE'S STORY OF
OUR HERITAGE

YOUNG PEOPLE'S
STORY OF
OUR HERITAGE

THE MEDIEVAL WORLD

by

V. M. HILLYER and E. G. HUEY

New Edition Designed and Revised by Childrens Press, Chicago

Consultants

William T. Nichol, Principal
Charles Gates Dawes Elementary School, Evanston, Illinois

John R. Lee, Professor of Education
Northwestern University, Evanston, Illinois

Meredith Press, New York

Illustrations in the order in which they appear

Library of Congress Catalog Card Number: 66-11330

Copyright © 1966 by Meredith Publishing Company. Originally published under the title of *A Child's History of the World* by V. M. Hillyer. Revised and enlarged Edition, with new material by Edward G. Huey. Copyright, 1924, by The Century Co. Copyright, 1947, by D. Appleton-Century Company, Inc. Copyright, 1951, by Appleton-Century-Crofts, Inc. Copyright, 1952 by Origineale Fletcher. All rights reserved. Printed in the U.S.A. Published simultaneously in Canada.

Contents

Acknowledgments

Cover painting, top: Pope Leo III
John Hollis—Hollis Associates

Cover painting, bottom: Madonna and Child, a painting by Verrocchio
Alpha Photo Service

Page 2: Interior of a Gothic Cathedral, typical of those built
during the Middle Ages
Bob Brunton—Hollis Associates

Frontis: A page from the Gutenberg Bible
Art Reference Bureau

Opposite: Chinese art objects like this pottery horse
found their way to the West after the Crusades
Courtesy of the Art Institute of Chicago

———————————

Designer: John Hollis

Project Editor: Joan Downing

Manuscript Editor: Frances Dyra

Editorial Staff: Mary Reidy, Gerri Stoller

THE MEDIEVAL WORLD

Introduction

The end of the Roman Empire in the West marked the end of Ancient History and the beginning of a new age. Historians call the next thousand years—from 500 A.D. to 1500 A.D.—the *Middle Ages* or the "medieval" world. The word medieval comes from a Latin word meaning "time in the middle." During this middle time there was a sharp break between the great gains of the ancient civilizations of Greece and Rome and the new rule of the barbarians. In fact, hundreds of years passed before the Western world came under an organized system of law and government that is the trademark of our modern world. The medieval world saw the end of many of the old ways and the beginning of the new world.

The first part of this middle period, from about 500 A.D. to 1000 A.D., is often called the *Dark Ages*. Historians use this name to describe the chaos and confusion that the barbarian invasions caused. The fall of Rome left no permanent government in the West. People were so busy fighting to protect themselves and their possessions that they had no time for anything else. As a result cities fell into ruin; businesses went broke; manufacturing and trade almost stopped; and without a steady government, no money was made nor laws enforced. People went back to the land. From this land they raised enough food for themselves and their families. And this was all the war-weary, poor people of the Dark Ages had time to do.

Then slowly things changed. The Crusades brought many new ideas into Europe. Towns began to grow and trades began to make items for sale. A middle class developed and became important. Slowly people of the world—a Christian World—began to develop and explore and discover things both old and new. They formed national states under absolute monarchs. The countries, the laws, and the learning of the later Middle Ages are reflected in our world today. Without the developments of this time our world would be very different from what it is.

The World of the Barbarians: The Western Roman Empire

The world governed by the barbarians was very different from the one ruled by Rome or Constantinople. The invading tribes divided the empire into bits and pieces. They ruled with force of arms. A tribe ruled a section of land absolutely—that is, without the consent or approval of the subject people. They could do—and often did do—anything they wanted to. A barbarian chief was limited only by the customs and traditions of his tribal code. No longer did the Roman system of law and government exist.

Because it ruled with force, a tribe could be driven out by a stronger enemy. When this happened, and it frequently did during the Dark Ages, the old group would fade away and a new one take over. This struggle for land and power went on during much of the Middle Ages.

Many different tribes settled in the West. The barbarians who went into Britain were known as the *Angles* and the *Saxons*. They overpowered and drove to the highlands the native Picts and Celts. This group of Angles and Saxons was very important. In fact, the country they took over bears their name. At first called "land of the angels," this eventually became Angle-land, and then what we call the country today—England. The people of England and their descendents are known as Anglo-Saxons.

Another powerful barbaric tribe called *Vandals* went into Gaul, where France is now. They were later forced into Spain where they continued stealing, smashing, and burning. They then crossed over by boat into Africa, injuring and destroying everything that stood in their way. So it is that today when anyone damages or destroys property wickedly, we call him a vandal.

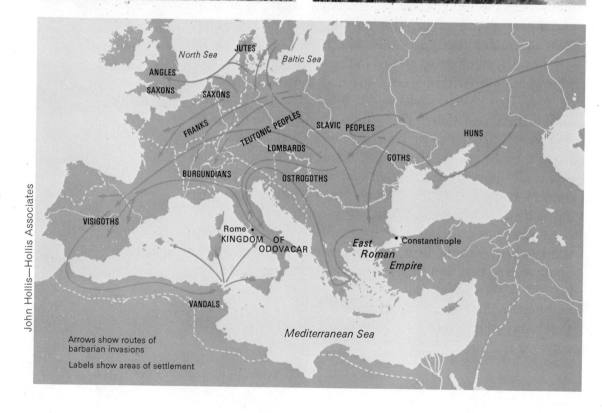

North Sea

JUTES

Baltic Sea

ANGLES

SAXONS

SAXONS

FRANKS

TEUTONIC PEOPLES

SLAVIC PEOPLES

HUNS

LOMBARDS

GOTHS

BURGUNDIANS

OSTROGOTHS

VISIGOTHS

Rome

KINGDOM OF ODOVACAR

East Roman Empire

Constantinople

VANDALS

Mediterranean Sea

Arrows show routes of
barbarian invasions

Labels show areas of settlement

Another of the most important and permanent tribes that invaded the Roman Empire was known as the *Franks*. This tribe followed the Vandals into Gaul. They settled down and under mighty rulers established a strong government. They gave the name "France" to the old Roman province of Gaul.

Many groups came to Italy. The *Visigoths* led by Alaric and the *Huns* under Attila came to Rome. But in the sixth century—the five hundreds—the *Ostrogoths* set up a government. They were overthrown by the victorious army of Justinian. When this last government fell, the Lombards ruled Italy for over two hundred years.

Although the barbarian tribes differed in many ways, they had many things in common. They were all uneducated. Unlike average Greeks and Romans, most of the newcomers —those that came in strength just before the fall of Rome in 476 A.D.—knew nothing at all about "book learning." They were very primitive people. They only knew their own ways which were very, very different from the cultural traditions of the Romans.

They did not speak the language of the Roman Empire— Latin. They could not even read or write in their own languages. And so they brought no written literature, art, or philosophy to the new land. In fact, because of their own lack of knowledge, they often destroyed or neglected the many valuable things they found.

They couldn't use the important things developed by the Romans, and so they didn't keep them up. Because they didn't speak Latin, schools, libraries, and books were not as important as gold ornaments or silk cloth. Also they didn't need the skills taught from these things. All their children had to know could be learned in the family. The boys had to learn how to fight, and the girls to make and grow the items needed to run their simple homes. They did not learn how to build magnificent buildings. They had no use for them. Their homes were very simple. Certain tribes

opposite, top left: A Frankish Warrior in battle dress

opposite, top right: Teuton homes. In the foreground is a food storehouse built on stilts to protect the contents from animals.

opposite bottom: Map showing the migration of barbarian tribes

lived in holes in the ground during the winter months and in simple tent-like structures during the summer. Because of the constant fighting and moving they didn't live in cities. Most tribes were able to carry off their possessions within minutes, if necessary. They didn't need to keep the excellent Roman roads in good repair because they only rode horses or walked from one place to another. They didn't make items to sell so they didn't need the roads to carry goods to market. So the famous Roman roads were neglected. The cities became unimportant and many of them disappeared.

The barbarians governed others with military strength. They governed themselves with their own tribal laws. So they had no use for the Roman system of law and government.

The Teutonic tribes had a very interesting legal system. They did not have written rules, but still they had a definite tribal law. Each person knew what he could or could not do. These rules were based on age-old tribal customs or ways. Most of the crimes were punished by the head of the family unit. Disputes did not go to the chief or king or the tribal assembly for a decision unless they were very important.

If someone hurt someone else, justice would be satisfied if the injured party was paid. This payment of money or goods was called *compensation*. For example, if a man broke another tribesman's leg he would have to pay a certain amount. This was called the *bots*. This made it easy for him, for he knew ahead of time what the price of his action would be. If he lost his temper and killed someone he had to pay more. This sum was called *wergeld*. To kill someone important like a chief or noble cost more than just killing a peasant.

Some crimes were considered *botless;* that is, payment would not be enough. Then a trial would be held. The Teutons had interesting trials. The man accused of the crime would bring all his friends to court. They would publically swear that the man was telling the truth about his innocence. If enough appeared to clear the man, he was set free. This system was called *compurgation*. The Teutons believed in compurgation because it was believed that the gods would punish anyone who swore falsely.

In another kind of trial the two people involved fought each other. It was thought that heaven would grant victory only to the party who was right, or innocent. This was the so-called "wager of battle or combat."

left: The Frankish custom of "Trial by Ordeal" lasted well into the Middle Ages

The last way in which the Teutons determined guilt or innocence was even stranger than the other ways. This was called the "trial by ordeal." The accused might have to put his hand into boiling water or carry a hot iron a certain distance or walk upon hot rocks. If after a few days he showed no bad sign—that is, a severe burn or infection—he was declared innocent.

Another ordeal was usually fatal. The accused was tied and thrown into a stream. If he floated he was innocent. If he sank he was guilty. Few sinners had a chance to survive this ordeal. Of course, few innocent men had a chance, either. Yet it must be remembered that no one in the tribe endured a trial by ordeal unless the chiefs were quite sure he was guilty in the first place.

The Teutons had an entirely different set of gods from those of the Greeks and Romans. The chief god of the Teutons, as you might guess, was the god of war, whom they called *Woden*. Woden was also the god of the sky. He was like the Roman gods Jupiter and Mars put together. Woden was supposed to live in a wonderful palace in the sky, in the heaven of dead warriors, called *Valhalla*. Many tales are told of the wonderful things Woden did and of the adventures he had. Wednesday, which was once "Wodensday," is named after him. That is why there is the letter "d" in this word, although we don't pronounce it.

After Woden, *Thor* was the next most important god. He was the god of lightning and thunder. Thor carried a hammer with which he fought great "ice giants" who lived in the far-off lands. Thursday, which was once "Thorsday," is named after him.

Another god was named *Tiu*, and from this name we get "Tuesday." From another, *Freya*, god of love, we get "Friday."

Sunday and Monday are named after the sun and moon, and Saturday is named after a Greek god, Saturn.

A Teuton thought the most important virtue was bravery or courage. No honorable barbarian could be a coward. Like the Spartans, it was expected that the warrior would never abandon his shield in battle. He would fight until death.

Barbarian tribes honored freedom. So often they elected their leaders, called kings. They were not kings because their fathers were kings before them, or because they had taken thrones by force. They were selected or elected by their fellow warriors who assembled for the purpose. They were often the most respected and most powerful men in the tribe. After his election a king ruled, but he often called his warriors together to discuss important things and hear trials.

In almost every tribe the warrior had a personal following. This included men, women, and children. Each pledged loyalty to the warrior. The men fought for him and with him. And in return the leader gave them food, shelter, and weapons. We shall see how this personal association or "pledge of loyalty" to one man affected later generations.

above: Frankish warriors celebrate the election of a new king

The Byzantine Empire: The Eastern Roman Empire

While the western portion of the Roman Empire appeared to be hurled back in time, the eastern part, at Constantinople, flourished. This city was perched on a peninsula jutting into the sea. Surrounded on three sides by water and protected by a strong wall in the rear, Constantinople was able to withstand the barbarian attacks. For a thousand years she successfully defended herself against her enemies.

Not long after the fall of Rome, Constantinople had one of her greatest emperors. His name was Justinian. He ruled the Eastern Roman Empire from 527 A.D. to 565 A.D.

Justinian was the son of a peasant family and he rose to power through the army. He was a Christian and spoke Latin. Theodora, his wife, was also of simple birth.

You might not believe that these two were wise enough to rule, but they ruled well. Pictures often show them together because, according to the records, Theodora often helped her husband make the right decisions.

When Justinian became emperor there were a great many things to be done. One of the first things he did concerned the law. Up to this time there had been many, many rules or laws by which the people were governed. It was often difficult for the people to know what they must do and what they must not do.

In order to untangle this snarl, Justinian hired a lawyer named Tribonian. He gathered together all the laws and all the judges' decisions that had been made in Roman courts since the Law of the Twelve Tables had been written hundreds of years before. This famous collection of law was put together into one big book and called *Corpus Juris Civilis*, the Body of Civil Law. We call this collection *Justinian's Code* because he was the man responsible for bringing it together. Many of these laws were so good and so just that they are still in use today. If you notice that Justinian begins with the word "just," this will help you remember that he was the emperor who made just laws.

In addition to organizing the law, Justinian also managed to run his government and his army in such a way that things never got out of control as they had in Rome. Certain men did certain jobs for the government and when an emperor died or a weak man ruled, these men continued to do their jobs. This type of governmental organization is called a *bureaucracy*. It had nothing to do with democracy. This simply means that each man checked on the one under him; so men continued to do their special jobs no matter what. This was very important because it kept Constantinople free.

Justinian was a devout Christian. To demonstrate his devotion he built a very beautiful church called Santa Sophia. Today it is no longer a church but a museum. You can still see this magnificent building if you visit the city of Constantinople, now called Istanbul.

Justinian did something that wasn't very good, however. He closed the famous school of philosophy at Athens that had been established by Aristotle and Plato and attended by the Stoics and Epicureans. He thought closing the school was good because he believed it taught pagan, or irreligious, ideas. Today we know these schools were more like universities. Their closing, along with the end of schools in the western part of the empire, slowed down learning for hundreds of years.

A very busy emperor, Justinian did something else that may surprise you. It had nothing to do with law, government, or buildings. It had to do with fashion and big business. Justinian was responsible for bringing the manufacture of silk to Europe. During his reign, two men who had lived in the land called Cathay for many years and knew how silk cloth was made, smuggled the answer into Constantinople. They brought with them a batch of silkworm eggs. They took care of them and showed workers how to make the silk cloth from the fine silk thread. This enabled the people to make fine silk clothes and fine silk ribbons. Justinian was also successful outside the empire. Through his long wars he was able to take Africa. He also regained part of Spain and, after a war that lasted twenty years, he recaptured Italy.

He successfully protected the borders of his empire from the barbarians from the north, and he stopped the Persians, the old enemies of the Greeks, from taking over territory around the eastern coast of the Mediterranean.

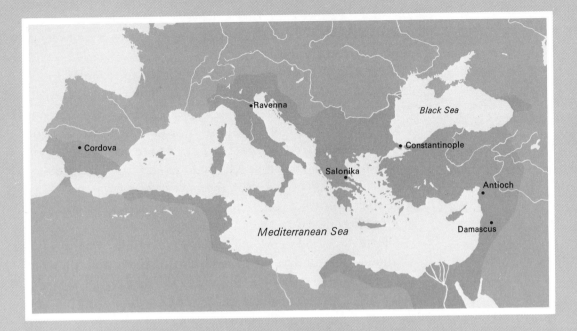

At no time however, did the Roman Empire of the East gain control of the northern parts of the old empire. The land in England, Gaul, and Germany remained under the rule of the barbarians. The successors of Justinian were unable to keep his gains, and before long Africa again fell into other hands. Italy, except for Rome, Ravenna, and some southern cities, also was conquered.

As time passed, the differences between the East and West increased. The languages were different, for after Justinian's death in 565, no eastern emperor spoke Latin. Greek became the official language of both the government and the church. In the West the people spoke a combination of the barbarians' native languages mixed with Latin. This, plus the difference in daily life and government, separated forever each part of the former empire.

above: The Byzantine Empire at the time of Justinian

Although it might not have seemed so at the time, the modern world has benefited much more from the contributions of the barbarians than it has from the civilization of the Byzantine empire. For although Constantinople lasted a long, long time she did not develop many new or important things. Her greatest gift was in protecting the past. It was to the West that the future belonged. In the coming centuries the major tribes settled down and combined the old and the new into a completely new way of life. Our story of the Middle Ages deals mostly with these newcomers.

Two Famous Kings

About the same time that Justinian lived, there was a king in Gaul (France) who became very important. His name was Clovis. He was the king of the Franks—a very large and important tribe.

King Clovis was one of the first barbarian rulers to enlarge his territory and rule it for a long time. He was a strong ruler. But this is not why he is important to our story. He is important because of what he became. King Clovis was the first barbarian king to become a Christian. Many of the barbarians who had settled in Rome earlier had become Christians. But the newcomers from the north and west were not Christians. Most of them, as we have said, still believed in their pagan gods.

Clovis married a woman named Clotilda who was a Catholic Burgundian princess. She disliked the fighting and cruelty of her people and when she discovered that the Christians did not believe in quarreling and fighting she decided to become a Christian.

When she married Clovis she tried to persuade him to become a Christian also. At first he would not listen. Then just before Clovis went into battle against a barbarian tribe—the Alamans—he promised God that if he won this battle he would become a Christian. He did win and in 496 he was baptized; and 3,000 of his warriors were baptized, too.

This was very important because other chiefs were pagans who had little in common with the people in this part of the old Roman Empire. The people felt that Clovis was more like them and they were more ready to accept his leadership and rule. Clovis made Paris his capital, and Paris is still the capital of France.

We would like to say that Clovis became a good and kind king. But he didn't. Unfortunately, he still acted like a rough, pagan barbarian. Clovis used his Christianity for earthly goals. He extended his control of the land through his constant wars—against Romans, Visigoths, Burgundians. He continued to kill and steal just as though he had never heard of the Christian ideas of love and peace.

Still this man is important to our story. His heirs—his sons and his sons' sons—ruled this land for about 200 years.

It was about this same time that a king named Arthur was ruling in England. Many stories and poems have been written about Arthur, and though they are very interesting, they are legends and not fact.

The most famous story was among the first tales written about King Arthur; it was written by an Englishman, Sir Thomas Malory, at the end of the Hundred Years' War. Called *Morte d'Arthur*, this story tells about Tristan and Lancelot, Arthur's most famous noble knights, and Merlin the magician, and Arthur's lovely queen, Guinevere.

One part of the legend of Arthur tells about a sword called Excalibur. This weapon was stuck so fast in a stone that no one could draw it out except the man who should be king of England. All the nobles of England tried without success to pull out the sword. But no one could. Then one day a young boy, Arthur, pulled out Excalibur with the greatest of ease, and according to the legend, immediately was proclaimed king.

King Arthur chose a company of nobles to rule with him. At his castle's court he and his nobles sat at a gigantic round table; because of this table they became known as the Knights of the Round Table. Tennyson, an English poet, wrote in verse an account of all the wonderful doings of King Arthur and his knights. They are all in a long poem called *The Idylls of the King*.

The baptism of Clovis, a great barbarian King

The Rise of Christianity

Throughout the history of mankind people have sought the good life. Every age has had different ideas about what this was. The Greeks thought that knowledge and beauty brought a good life. The Stoics thought "not caring" was good. The Epicurians thought living wisely and nobly and seeking good should be the goal of all men. Even the Teutons thought that courage and bravery in battle was good.

All these people believed in the "here and now." Their different gods and different religious beliefs centered on this life. Christianity was different. Christianity taught people that this life wasn't all-important. It said that life after death—the life that wouldn't end, eternity—was the highest goal. Men worked hard to earn this eternal life. During the Middle Ages we will see how people lived and worked, not for now but for the rewards that would come after death.

Before the invasions of the fifth century, Christianity had spread. Since the time of Constantine in the three hundreds, it was actively supported by the Roman government. The barbarians of the later centuries weren't Christians, of course. But, by the twelfth century—the 1100's—most people in Europe were members of the Roman Catholic Church.

At first the organization of the church was simple. Men went from place to place teaching and instructing converts. Then, leaving someone in charge, they went on. But as time passed a more complicated system developed. Certain important men called *bishops* came to be looked upon as the heads of particular areas. They made many decisions for

Early Christian
missionary

their section. By the sixth century there were important bishops in Rome, Antioch, Constantinople, Alexandria, and Jerusalem. Each had about equal authority. Under these bishops were the *priests* who conducted church services and married, baptized, and buried church members. Under the priests were the church members. Whether king or peasant, all people were subject to the guidance and rule of the church.

At this time, the Catholic Church became the only stable thing in the lives of the people in the West. As we have mentioned, the barbarian governments that took over after 476 did not always last long. So for about the next five hundred years it was the church to whom many people

23

Alinari—Art Reference Bureau

Because of his strong leadership, Pope Gregory I was called Gregory the Great

turned. The church in Rome became more and more important. She gave not only spiritual comfort but also earthly comfort. Law, education, help for the sick and poor, and many other things previously handled by the Roman Government, were now done by the church.

The bishop of Rome began to be looked upon as the sole head of the whole church. At first the other bishops objected, but eventually they agreed to accept his rule. The supremacy of the bishop at Rome was based on several things. Perhaps the most important point was the fact that both Peter and Paul had once lived there and that Peter had founded the church there. This made Rome the home of the first of the great church leaders. Another important point was the fact that Rome was once the capital of the entire Mediterranean world. And, although her power was gone, Rome's former greatness was remembered. And last, but not least, the church at Rome became the leader because of a series of great leaders.

The leader of the church even today resides in Rome. He is called the pope. At first this word, which in Latin was *papa*, was used to describe all bishops and priests. But as the power of the bishop of Rome grew, pope came to be used only for the one head of the church.

One of the early, outstanding popes was Gregory I. He did much for the church and for the world. He was a writer, a statesman, an organizer, and a missionary. In this last role he sent men to convert the barbarians in Germany and England. These conversions were done primarily by a special group of religious men called *monks*.

Monks and Monasteries

Most men lead good lives by living according to their beliefs and being honest and kind to others in their everyday life. Some good people, however, both Christian and non-Christian, withdrew from the world. They often went to a solitary place by themselves to pray and meditate about God and goodness. They frequently fasted, which means they ate very simple food and only enough to keep them alive. These people were called *hermits*.

One of the strangest hermits was named St. Simeon Stylites. He built a pillar, or column, fifty feet high. On the top of it he built a platform with only enough room to sit or stand. He could not lie down. He lived on the top of the pillar for many years, day and night, winter and summer, while the sun shone on him and the rain rained on him. He never came down. He could be reached only by a ladder, which his friends used to bring him food and water. High up out of the world, he thought he could best lead a holy life. That was his idea of "being good." Some think such a person would do more for mankind if he "did something."

Not all people who wanted to fast and pray were hermits. Others who wanted to lead holy lives began to gather and live in groups. These groups of Christian men were called monks. This word comes from the Latin word *monachus*, which in turn came from the Greek word *monos*, meaning alone. Monks, both in the East and the West, became very important in the Middle Ages, and their homes, or *monasteries*, came to play a vital role in the many developments of this age.

In the sixth century a man named Benedict lived in Rome where he saw many people living wild and cruel lives. He was unhappy with this and left the city to live alone as a hermit. People became impressed with this "holy" man Benedict and many young men came to join him. Finally he built a building on the top of a mountain in Italy. This ancient building, called Monte Cassino, was bombed during World War II, but has since been rebuilt. It is still a Benedictine monastery. Monks still live there— more than 1100 years after Benedict founded it.

Monte Cassino, founded by Benedict, still stands in Italy

Benedict knew that people had to have rules to follow to help them lead "good" lives. So he wrote down a set of rules. These worked so well at Monte Cassino that many other monasteries copied them. Today Benedict's Rule and the others based on it are used in monasteries all over the world.

According to this rule, men who wanted to become monks had to make three solemn promises, or vows. The first was to promise never to own anything, not even a spoon. This was the vow of *poverty*. Monks also promised never to marry and live pure lives. This was the vow of *chastity*. The last vow was their solemn promise to forget what they themselves might want and always to obey without question what the head of their monastery told them to do. This was their vow of *obedience*.

The head of a monastery was called an *abbot*. He was elected by his fellow monks, but after his election he ruled absolutely. He might call an assembly of his monks and ask their opinion but when he decided what to do he did it all by himself. All the monks in the abbey or monastery had to obey him. The abbot ruled until his death. Most of the abbots were good men. They were wise and ruled their abbeys like good fathers rule their houses, rewarding, helping, commanding, and punishing whenever necessary.

Benedict also believed that men must work if they were to be holy. So in addition to the three promises they made, his monks agreed to follow a daily plan. This plan organized every minute of every monk's day.

Certain times were set aside for prayer and physical labor. Work was considered a prayer—whether it was gardening, washing dishes, or sweeping floors. They worked in honor of God.

Much of the work was done on the land that surrounded the monastery building. Often it was barren or swampy land. Sometimes this land belonged to no one. Other times it was given to the monks by some wealthy lord who wished to gain church favor at a cost that was not too great. These lords often gave land that was not good, or even worse than that, land that was dangerously unhealthy.

But the monks worked hard. They drained the swampy land, watered the dry land, and tilled the soil. They often made waste places fertile again. In fact, the monasteries were often like model farms, places people could visit to learn about the best ways to treat soil and grow crops.

right: A monk tills a field near his monastery

opposite, top left: Beautiful artwork was used on illuminated manuscripts of the Middle Ages

opposite, top right: Many people were interested in astronomy. This chronicle shows the phases of the moon.

opposite bottom: An illustrated section of a botany book

Monasteries raised cattle and sheep, vegetables for their table, and fodder for the animals. The monks, like most of the people in the early Middle Ages, raised or made everything they needed.

Perhaps the most important job they did was copying books. Remember, printing had not been invented and all books had to be written by hand. The monks copied ancient manuscripts, written in Latin and Greek, on calfskin or sheepskin called *vellum*. This material was much stronger than paper and lasted much longer. Thus, the monks of the Middle Ages kept much of the literature of the past for future generations.

These "hand-written" manuscripts are considered the art treasures of the Middle Ages. That is because many were beautifully illuminated, or decorated. Usually the first letter on each page or chapter heading was a large, colorfully designed capital letter. Often the borders were decorated with detailed designs of flowers, vines, birds, and other pictures in green, gold, blue, and red.

In addition to the copying of books the monks also left the world their own type of history. This was largely found in diaries and records of the various monasteries. Here are recorded the day to day and year to year events of the area.

28

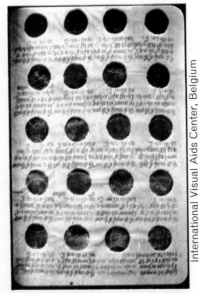

These old records are called *chronicles*. They are very important because without them we would not know what went on. You must remember that the Teutonic tribes could not read or write at first, and so they left few if any written records.

The monks were the best-educated people of their day. And as time passed, monasteries became the only schools in the Middle Ages. They taught both young and old the things they knew. The most important subjects were reading and writing. Monastery schools were not like today's

deo salutari nro. ps. veni

lxy? Nocte surgentes.

vt non delinq; ps dauid.

quam in lingua mea.

Poliu ori meo custodi

aim conlistet peccator a

schools. Almost everything they taught had to do with religion. Reading was very limited. Still, they kept the desire for learning alive and in later years the great universities developed and in the later Middle Ages took over teaching.

Perhaps you think that with all this the monks were doing enough—but they did even more. For the common people of the time the monasteries were also inns. Anyone who asked for lodging or shelter was given food and a place to sleep, whether he had money or not. For, as Benedict had said and as others practiced, every traveler was to be received as if he were Christ.

The monks also helped the poor and needy. The sick, too, came to the monastery to be treated and taken care of. Many people who had received such help or attention made rich gifts to monasteries. These gifts, plus the products of their land, made some monasteries very wealthy. Although the monks could not own anything themselves, things could belong to the building. These were passed down from generation to generation.

The monks also added another job to their list. It was their task to convert the barbarians to Christianity. To do this, monks were sent by their abbot to other parts of the world. One of the earliest and most famous missionaries was St. Patrick, who was sent to Ireland and who is considered the Irish patron saint. According to Irish legend, he performed a great act. He drove the snakes out of Ireland and thus convinced the Celtic tribal chiefs of the power of Christianity.

Another monk, Augustine, was sent to England. He managed to become friendly with a local chief and was given land in Canterbury. This land today is headquarters of a magnificent cathedral and the Church of England. Another famous monk was sent to Germany. His name was Boniface. He dared to cut down a tree said to be sacred to a pagan god without suffering any punishment. This so influenced the onlookers that they adopted Christianity. Hundreds of other monks spread Christianity, established monasteries, and brought developments in literature, learning, and agriculture to barbarian tribes throughout the world.

opposite: Elaborate designs were used around capital letters in illuminated Bibles

Mohammed

above: Head of Mohammed, who was called the Messenger of Allah

opposite: The Hegira, Mohammed's secret flight

In the seventh century a new religion developed that changed the world. As we have said, all the Byzantine emperors ruling after Justinian spoke Greek and used this language in their religion and government. The eastern empire maintained either direct control or indirect influence on the eastern and southeastern shores of the Mediterranean. These lands had for centuries shared the Greek and Roman traditions because they had been ruled or influenced at different times by each nation. But this relationship was dramatically changed.

This old unity disappeared, and the Mediterranean was separated into two armed camps.

A few years after the death of Justinian, in 570, a boy was born to a poor family that roamed the desert lands of Arabia. He was named Mohammed. Left an orphan at an early age, Mohammed had to work hard to stay alive. He probably had very little schooling and probably couldn't even write.

Mohammed went to work with the caravans and traders that carried the riches of the East to the coast to be sold in other parts of the world. Thus he came in contact with the beliefs of both the Christians and the Jews. After his marriage to a lady of wealth, he became a successful businessman in the city of Mecca.

As time passed, Mohammed became convinced that his fellow Arabs were wrong to worship many gods and idols. There was only one God who was all powerful. His name in Arabic was *Allah.*

At first Mohammed told only his family and friends of his beliefs. They believed him and accepted his new faith. When Mohammed was forty, one day he went to a cave to think and pray. There, it is said, he had a vision. The Angel Gabriel appeared to him and told him that God wanted him to go and teach all his fellow Arabs about his religion. Mohammed was God's prophet, as Moses had been.

Mohammed did as he had been directed. But although his wife and friends accepted his teachings, others did not. They laughed at him at first and began to think he was very dangerous. A group of his enemies in Mecca attempted to kill him. Fortunately, Mohammed heard of their plot and he fled the city with his family and friends. He went to the town of Medina in 622 to continue his work, and here he was very successful.

This flight from Mecca to Medina was called in Arabic the *Hegira* (heh-jye'rah), which means "flight." All those who believe in the teachings of Mohammed use 622 as the Year One of their calendar. Much the same as all Christians use the year of Christ's birth as the Year One of their calendar.

After the Hegira, Mohammed was very successful. The people of Medina accepted him and became his followers. When his city of Mecca saw him again, just six years later, it was as a general leading a great army. He captured Mecca and began converting his Arab tribesmen to the new religion. By the time he died in 632 A.D., Mohammed had converted almost all the Arabs.

This new religion was called *Islam*, which means submission in Arabic. Those who followed this religion were called *Moslems* or *Muslims* or *Mohammedans*, which means one who has submitted. We shall refer to Mohammed's followers as Moslems.

As we have mentioned, Mohammed probably couldn't read or write well. However, many of his words—which came from his visions or from his messages from God—were collected after his death and combined into one palm-leaf book. This is the Bible of the Moslems and it is called the *Koran*. It tells faithful Moslems what they can and cannot do.

Because Mohammed was born in Mecca, this is the sacred city of the Mohammedans. Each good Moslem tries to travel to Mecca at least once in his lifetime, no matter how far away he lives. A religious trip of this type is called a *pilgrimage*.

The Moslems worship in a building called a *mosque*. Good Moslems are required to pray, facing Mecca, five times each day. The call to pray is given by a man called a *muezzin* (mue-ezz'in). He stands on a little balcony on the minaret of the mosque. In a loud voice he calls: "Come to prayer; come to prayer. There is but one God and he is Allah." Then no matter where a Moslem is or what he is doing, whether he is in the street, at the marketplace, or working or playing, he must face toward Mecca, fall on his knees, bow his head and hands toward the ground and pray. Because he is required to do this no matter what, a Moslem sometimes carries a small rug called a prayer rug with him so that he may have something holy to kneel on.

The Moslems do not ignore the writings of the Old Testament, but they do not believe that Jesus was divine. They believe he was a prophet and that Mohammed was his successor, the last and greatest prophet. A good Moslem says, "There is one God, Allah, and Mohammed is his prophet."

The *Koran* tells the Moslems to do many other things. They must give alms to the poor. They must not eat pork or drink wine. They must obey the rules of Mohammed if

above: The muezzin calls believers to prayer

they are to gain paradise. They must fast during the daylight hours of the ninth month, called *Ramadan*. And finally, all believers in Mohammed and his teachings are one body no matter what tribe or race or rank they have in this life.

The last point is very important in our story, for this did much to unite the Arabs into one force. Before this time the Arab tribes had been independent nomads traveling and living in the arid climate of Arabia. Now they had a common bond, plus the burning desire to spread the faith of Mohammed.

At first the Moslems tried to persuade others to join simply by talking to them and telling them how fine their religion was. But very soon the Moslems began to use force. This may seem like a strange way to convert people, but the Moslems believed they were right. Allah wanted all people to believe in him and become Moslems. Also Mohammed had said that a Moslem who died fighting for his faith against the "unbelievers" would automatically gain a high place in paradise. This sounds very familiar doesn't it? Remember that the Christians also thought death for their faith was very good.

And so it was not long after the death of Mohammed that the Arabs began to conquer more and more lands. Under Abu Bekr, who was Mohammed's successor, the new religion spread.

The leaders of the Moslems were called *caliphs*. Under Abu Bekr the Moslems conquered Palestine. Led by the caliph Omar, Moslems took Egypt and Syria, including Jerusalem and the Holy Land, from the weak Eastern Empire. On the place where the Temple of Solomon once stood Omar built a mosque. This building still stands today in Jerusalem.

The Arabs, or Saracens as they are also called, kept moving northward toward Europe, traveling up the eastern coast of the Mediterranean Sea. They conquered and converted people to Islam as they went. Nothing could stop them. Their lightning-like border raids revealed how weak the empire of Byzantium was. By 650 A.D., less than eighteen years after the death of Mohammed, Persia fell to the Saracens. Now the only power left was Constantinople. Here the emperor ruled his Christian people. This was also the gateway from Asia to Europe, and the Arabs had to get by it if they were to continue their march. But the Christians, led by Emperor Leo III, poured down red-hot tar and burning oil from the walls of this fortified city. Despite their desperate attacks, the Arabs were forced to stop. They could not capture the city. The Byzantine victory in this battle that occurred in 717 saved eastern Europe. This land remained Christian, and free from Moslem rule.

However, this defeat did not stop the Arabs. They now went westward. Moving around the Mediterranean, they crossed Egypt, which was converted to Islam. They moved across the coast of Africa until only the strait of Gibraltar separated them from Spain, their first step into Europe.

Spain at this time was ruled by the Vandal tribe and there was no strong central government. When the Arabs crossed the strait in boats, carrying their weapons and their swift Arabian stallions, the people of Spain were unable to stop them. The Arabs were able to march up Spain and cross the Pyrenees into Gaul.

It seemed they soon would conquer all of Europe and make the whole civilized world Moslem.

Finally, near the town of Tours in France, they met organized resistance. The king of France at this time was a descendent of Clovis. Like his ancestor, he was Christian. But unlike his mighty ancestor, this king was weak. In

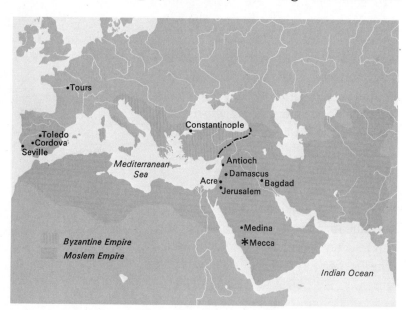

above: The Moslem Empire

opposite: The Franks, led by Charles Martel, defeated the Moslems at Tours

fact, for years the kings of this line had not bothered to rule their territory. They left this job to their right-hand men, who were called Mayors of the Palace. At the time of the Moslem invasion the Mayor of the Palace was a mighty man named Charles Martel. Because of his ability to strike terrific blows with his hammer, Charles was nicknamed Charles the Hammer. (Throughout this period of history kings and other famous men are often identified by their first name together with a nickname. This second name often described the person's most outstanding characteristic—either his appearance or his ability. So throughout the Middle Ages men had such names as Charles the Bald, Peter the Fat, and so on.)

To meet the invaders, Charles the Hammer marched his soldiers to Tours. He planned his defense cleverly. Unlike the Moslems, Charles did not have horses. He and his army fought on foot. This battle was to be a clash between infantry and cavalry. He had his men form a solid square. When the Moslem horsemen attacked this solid block of men, they couldn't budge it. They attacked again and again. As one Spanish writer described the scene, "the Franks stood like a wall of ice, shoulder to shoulder, cutting down Moors who attacked their line." Unable to break the line, the Moslems retired from the battle scene. They never again attempted to go farther into France. Europe was saved! This battle of Tours was in 732, just 110 years after the Hegira and only fifteen years after the Moslem defeat at Constantinople.

Still the accomplishments of the Moslems, or Mohammedans, in the short span of 110 years was almost unbelievable. They had conquered land from the Byzantine Empire on the northeast side of the Mediterranean all the way around the southern edge and far into Spain. Most of the people south and east of the Mediterranean are still followers of the Moslem religion.

---

opposite: Charles Martel was called Charles the Hammer

Arab Achievements

The Moslems had tried to enter Europe. Burning tar and oil had stopped them at Constantinople. Charles the Hammer stopped them at Tours. And Europe was saved. Yet when we examine the tremendous accomplishments of the Moslem Arabs we may wonder if Europe was so lucky. For from about 600 to 1000, most of the great achievements were made by the Arabic civilization.

The Arabs were appreciative of what they found in other lands. They were very good at adapting and using and extending the things they learned.

Mathematics and science were to benefit greatly from the Arab scholars. It was the Arabs who invented, used, and spread throughout their world the numerals we use today. 1, 2, 3, 4 and so on are called Arabic numerals. These eventually replaced the awkward Roman numerals such as V, X, D, C, which in Arabic numerals are 5, 10, 50 and 100. Roman numerals are still used today for some things, but they are not used in mathematics.

Moslem scholars made many advances in science. They began the science of chemistry. The scientists of this time were called *alchemists* (al'keh-mists). They believed that they could combine certain metals with other ingredients and make precious metals. These sought-after metals were usually either gold or silver. Alchemists also believed they could find a magic powder that would preserve human life, an idea that has frequently been the goal of men. They did discover and use many chemicals, such as sal ammonia, carbonate of soda, and cream of tartar.

The Moslems were the leading doctors of the time. While in the West sick people were treated with homemade remedies and superstition, in the Middle East doctors helped advance medicine by relearning the works of great Greek and Indian doctors. Two of the most famous doctors were Rhazes, who wrote an encyclopedia of medicine, and Avicenna, who wrote a book used until the sixteenth century.

Perhaps in the study of geography the Moslems made some of the greatest contributions. They used mathematics and in their tables used longitude and latitude to show position. They wrote many, many books about geography describing the land and the people. They made many maps. Their maps show Mecca as the center of the world while the Christian maps of the same period showed Jerusalem as the center. This shows how important religious feeling was.

The Moslems needed to know geography because their empire was very large. Their trade and commerce reached from the lands of Africa in the West into China in the East. Ships had no instruments and sailors used the sun and stars to guide them. Unless they had fair weather they did not dare to go beyond the sight of land. If they did, they ran the risk of being hopelessly lost at sea. It was hundreds of years before the compass was discovered to change this situation.

The Arabs built many beautiful buildings that were quite different from the Greek and Roman buildings. The doors and window-openings, instead of being square or round, were usually horseshoe-shaped. On the top of their mosques (churches) they built domes shaped something like an onion, and at the corners they put tall spires, or *mina-rets*, from which the *muezzin* could call aloud the hour of prayer. They covered the walls of their buildings with beautiful mosaics and designs. However, the *Koran* ruled that no decoration could be "any likeness of anything that is in heaven above, or that is in the earth beneath, or that is

An astrolabe. When the sky was clear, early Arab sailors determined their position at sea by observing the position of the sun or the stars with a primitive version of this instrument.

in the water under the earth." To keep this rule, Moslems never made drawings or pictures of any living thing, neither of plants nor flowers nor animals. They made designs using lines and curves. These lines were called *arabesques*, and they were often very beautiful.

Legend says that in Arabia there grew a little bush on which were small berries with seeds inside. The sheep liked these berries and, when they ate them, became very lively. The Arabs themselves tried eating the seeds of these berries and found they had the same effect on them. Then they made a drink out of these seeds by roasting and grinding them and boiling them in water. They called this *gahwah*, and from this Arabic word we get the English word coffee. The custom of drinking coffee spread first to Turkey and then to Italy. Today coffee is drunk all over the world.

The Arabs, like the Babylonians before them, found out that when the juice of grapes or other fruits or grains spoiled, or fermented, a change took place. They called the new thing to which these juices changed, "alcohol," and they were so much afraid of it and what it did to those who drank it that they forbade every Moslem to drink anything containing alcohol.

Woolen cloth which people used for clothes was made from the hair of sheep or goats. This kind of cloth was expensive, so the Arabs found out a way of making cloth from the cotton plant, which, of course, was much cheaper. Then in order to decorate the cloth and make it pretty, they stamped the plain cloth with wooden blocks shaped in different forms and dipped in color. This printed cloth that the Arabs had invented was called *calico*.

The Arabs made swords and knives of such wonderful steel that the blades could be bent double without breaking. These blades were so sharp they could cut through the finest

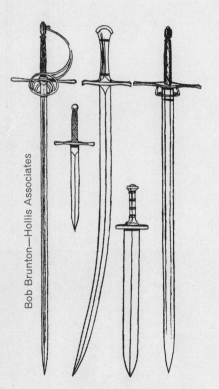

opposite, top right: Courtyard showing delicate carvings of Moslem architecture

opposite, top left: Gateways also were carved

opposite middle: Casbah of Taourirt. Casbahs were forts or walled parts of a city built for protection.

opposite bottom: Karaouive Mosque was an intellectual center during the Middle Ages

right: Toledo and Damascus swords not only were good weapons, but also were beautiful works of art

43

hair, and yet at the same time so strong that they could cut through a bar of steel. Such swords were made in the East at Damascus, in Syria, and in the West at Toledo, which is in Spain; these swords and knives were known as Damascus or Toledo blades. Unfortunately, no one knows the Arab's secret for making such marvelous blades. It is what is called a lost art.

Near where Babylon once stood, the Arabs, in about 750, built a magnificent city named Baghdad. You have heard of it if you have ever read any of the Arabian Nights, stories about Aladdin and his Lamp, Ali Baba and the Forty Thieves, or Sinbad the Sailor. For most of these stories were first told in Baghdad to entertain the caliph, Haraun-al-Raschid (hah-roon' ahr-rah-shed'). Today this former eastern capital of the Moslems is located in Iraq.

At Baghdad the Arabs built a great school that was famous for many, many years. At Cordova in Spain, the western capital of the Moslems, they built another great school. They also invented the game of chess, made the first clocks with pendulums, and started wonderful libraries of books. You can see what intelligent people they were.

After the death of Mohammed, Moslem rule, both religious and political, passed to a caliph. He made no new laws because the sacred law of the land was the *Koran*.

Like the other empires, the new Arab empire was divided into provinces. The caliph was supreme. Eventually this position became hereditary—that is, the job passed from father to son.

But the caliphs were not always good, strong, or capable rulers so after awhile, this one great empire divided into three parts or *caliphates*. These were Baghdad, Cairo, and Cordova.

clockwise from above:

The Court of the Lions, part of the Alhambra Palace

The Comares Tower and Basin of the Courtyard of the Myrtles, Granada

Outside walls of the Mosque at Cordova

The Alhambra Palace, residence of the Moorish kings

Charlemagne

The height of the Arab civilization occurred during the eighth, ninth, and tenth centuries. But this was in Asia and Africa, not Europe. What was happening in the part of Europe untouched by the Arabic religion or culture?

You will recall that the Franks were one of the most important barbarian tribes. Under their first strong leader, Clovis, they formed a fairly steady government. Unfortunately, the heirs of Clovis were not very strong rulers. They fought among themselves many times and divided the land which today includes West Germany and France. For two hundred years this fighting went on. The Frankish rulers became weaker, more disagreeable, and lazier. Soon the business of running the government passed to a chief official called the mayor of the palace, or Major Domus.

We mentioned one of the outstanding mayors of the palace. He was Charles the Hammer who defeated the Moslems at Tours. The son of Charles the Hammer succeeded his father as mayor of the palace. He was named Pepin the Short. Pepin was not happy because as mayor he did all the work while the lazy king had all the fun. So Pepin asked the most important man he knew, the bishop of Rome, who should be the real king. Remember, because there was no nationwide government for such a long time, the pope had become powerful and he could influence people in matters other than religion. The pope said it was Pepin who should be king. And so it was. Pepin founded a new ruling family in France called the Carolingians. From this family came the brightest light in the Dark Ages.

Upon the death of Pepin in 768, his son Charles took the throne. With his might and power Charles joined the pieces of Europe together once again.

The French name for Charles was Charlemagne. When he became king Charlemagne ruled France, but this was not enough for him. He began a series of battles and conquests against the barbarians on the western side of his empire, now part of Germany.

opposite: The consecration of Pepin the Short

Teuton warrior equipped
for battle

Pope Leo III ruled a strip of land that had been given to him by Charlemagne's father. He was having trouble protecting his land against the savage Lombards in the northern part of Italy. So he asked Charlemagne to help him. Charlemagne agreed and in fierce battles he defeated the Lombards and took over their land.

The pope, grateful to Charlemagne, wanted to reward him. So when Charlemagne paid a visit to the Church of St. Peter on Christmas Day in 800, the pope stepped suddenly from the altar and placed a crown on Charlemagne's head. Then raising his voice, Pope Leo proclaimed Charlemagne Emperor of the Romans. With this act, the pope gave his permission for a new empire. This act was a "first." In the later Middle Ages it caused trouble between the church and the state, but at this time the authority of the pope went unquestioned.

Charlemagne—a Teuton—now ruled this new Roman Empire. As ruler of an empire, Charlemagne was able to make many changes. Most of these were good.

He moved the capital of his empire from Paris to a place in Germany called Aachen, or Aix-la-Chapelle. This was more conveniently situated in the center of his large empire. Unlike earlier Teutons, Charlemagne had a great respect for education. He was curious to know everything and wanted his people to know everything. In 789 he passed a law that every monastery had to have a school. He was the first government official to do so since the fall of Rome. He also established a Palace School at his capital. Here the young people at court learn to read and write Latin, a skill long since lost by most people outside the monasteries.

The schools taught reading, writing, science, poetry, and especially Latin grammar and rhetoric. Charlemagne listened to the teachers and he learned many things. But he had a very hard time learning to read and write. Although he finally learned to read a little, he was never able to write anything more than his name. Despite this handicap, Charlemagne was one of the best-educated rulers in Europe at the time.

Much of what we know about Charlemagne was written by his secretary, Einhard, who wrote a biography of Charlemagne and the Frankish empire he ruled.

We know, for example, that although his daughters were princesses, Charlemagne made them learn how to weave, sew, and make clothes. He had them learn how to keep house and cook.

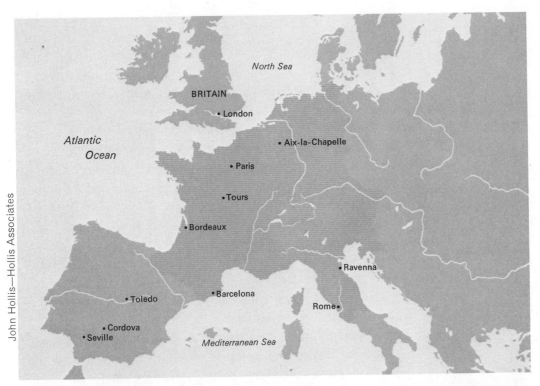

top: The empire controlled by Charlemagne

bottom: The cathedral at Aix-la-Chapelle was founded by Charlemagne and rebuilt in the tenth century. The tomb of Charlemagne is inside.

We also know that Charlemagne liked simple food and dress. He did not like obvious displays of any kind. A story is told about how Charlemagne once taught a lesson to his nobles who loved to wear fancy costumes. One day he took them hunting—a favorite sport of warriors—while a storm was in progress. Needless to say, the fancy clothes did not protect the men from the storm. In fact, you can imagine how silly they looked in their silks and ruffles after being caught in the rain.

Charlemagne divided his empire into *counties*. Each county was under the leadership of a man called a *count*. The counts swore loyalty to Charlemagne. Each one promised to represent Charlemagne in the country, to help raise armies and supplies, administer laws, collect taxes, and watch over the royal lands.

Charlemagne knew the counts might be tempted to serve themselves first and the empire second. To prevent this, he appointed men called the King's Messengers to check on the counts in the different areas. These men reported directly to Charlemagne on how his counts were ruling.

When Charlemagne died in 814, his kingdom was strong. His son, called Louis the Pious, inherited the kingdom. But, unfortunately, he lacked his father's ability to control. Upon his death in 840, the land was divided among his sons according to tradition. They fought each other for the land until the Treaty of Verdun was signed in 843. According to this agreement, Charles the Bald got the western part of the land, Ludwig the German got the eastern section, and Lothar got the title "Roman Emperor of the West" with a strip of land that ran from the North Sea south to Italy, between the east and west sections of his brothers' land.

But within fifty years this empire again completely disappeared, for a new series of barbarian invasions disrupted the land. Saracens (Moslems) attacked Italy. A tribe called Magyars (mag′ yahrz), as savage as the Huns, rode out from the East to terrorize the land. A branch of the Teuton family from the North, called the Northmen, plundered the land and later settled on the bits and pieces they carved from the empire of Charlemagne.

Alfred the Great

At one time, England had been governed by Romans. But after 407 there was no central ruler. It was an unimportant little island, ruled by the barbarian Saxons, Angles, and Jutes until the ninth century.

About sixty years after Charlemagne, in 871, there was a king of England named Alfred. England at this time was troubled by pirates. These pirates were cousins of the English—a tribe called Danes or Northmen. The English long ago had become Christians and civilized, but their cousins, the Danes from Scandinavia, were still rough and wild. They were large, strong men who fought with long-handled axes. They came over from their own country across the water in long boats moved by crude sails and oars. They landed on the coast of England, robbed the towns and villages, and then sailed back to their homes carrying off everything valuable they could lay their hands on. These raids were so bad that Saxon people used to pray, "From the fury of the Northmen, O Lord, deliver us . . .".

At last the Danes became so bold that they did not run away after robbing the country. They landed in the north-eastern section of England. In 866, the king's armies went out to punish these pirates, but instead of beating them, they themselves were beaten. It began to look as if these Danes might conquer the English completely.

Alfred decided that the best way to fight the Danes was not on land but on water, so he set to work building boats bigger and better than those the Danes had. After awhile he had something of a fleet, and the boats he built *were* bigger than those of the Danes, but they were so big they could not go into shallow water without running aground. The Danes' boats, on account of their small size, could go safely close into shore. In deep water, however, Alfred's fleet was strong and powerful. This was the first English navy. England's navy, which was to become the largest in the world, was started by Alfred the Great more than a thousand years ago.

above: The Saxon king, Alfred the Great

After fighting with the Danes for seven years, Alfred finally thought it best to make an agreement with them. In 878 the Danes promised to live in only one section of England and leave the part called Wessex alone. The king of the Danes, King Guthrum, became a Christian. For awhile there was peace, but several years later the Danes attacked again. Alfred was ready for them and beat them again and again. Finally the Danes fled Wessex in 886 and went to East Anglia and Northumbria in the eastern part of England and across to France.

Alfred was the king of England except for the parts ruled by Danish lords. He ruled Wessex and did many things during the time of peace. He made very strict laws and severely punished those who did wrong. Indeed, it is said that the people of England were so careful to obey the law during his reign that one might leave gold by the roadside and no one would steal it. He organized a successful army and navy.

Alfred also brought learned men from Europe to show his people how to make things and to teach them how to read and write. He translated Latin books into English. He also began writing a book telling about the events of his time. This was called the *Anglo-Saxon Chronicle*. So successful was this book that after Alfred's death people kept it up-to-date until the twelfth century. It is the best book historians have about this time in English history.

Alfred, king of England, is one of the outstanding men in history, but not just because of the land he ruled or his military victories. He was great because he was a noble man, a scholar, and a patriot. He is the only English king honored by being called the "Great."

Northmen raid the coast of England

Historical Pictures Service, Chicago

A.E.WOOD. SC.

Chaos and Confusion

Five hundred years passed, and most of these years were lawless times. There was fighting between lords. Invasions of Moslems and Danes disrupted all attempts at maintaining order.

The people who lived in the tenth century thought the Bible said something that meant the world was coming to an end in the year 1000, which was called the *millennium* from the Latin word meaning a thousand years.

Some people were glad the world was coming to an end. They were so poor and miserable and unhappy that they were anxious to go to heaven, where everything would be fine and lovely—if they had been good. So they were particularly good and did everything they could to earn a place for themselves in heaven.

Others were not so anxious to have the world come to an end. But, they thought, if it were coming to an end so soon, they might as well hurry up and enjoy themselves here while they still had a chance.

The year 1000 came, and nothing happened. As time went on, without any change, people began to think the end was delayed for some reason they could not explain. But it was not to be for many years after the millennium that people came at last to realize that the world was not going to end after all.

At this time, when the people of Europe were looking for the end of the world, there came another overwhelming series of invasions. Danger surrounded the struggling Christian civilizations. From the south and east the Moslem raiders attacked and conquered. From the northeast the Slavs threatened the boundaries of the Byzantine Empire. And from the plains of Asia Minor the Magyars, so like the tribesmen of Attila they were called Huns, threatened the remainder of Charlemagne's empire. But of all these dangers the most terrifying attacks were made by the Northmen, cousins of the tribe that had threatened England in the ninth century. Now they came again—raiding, killing, and plundering. One group under Canute conquered England completely. Others raided the seacoast towns of Europe and Italy, sometimes settling down but more often just destroying and plundering the land. These Northmen were called Normans, Norsemen, or Vikings. They were

opposite top: Gaul was plundered by the Northmen

opposite bottom: Ninth-century invasion routes of the Magyars, Vikings, Huns, and Moslems

ICELAND

Atlantic Ocean

NORWAY

Vikings

Novgorod

Vikings

North Sea

SWEDEN

Vikings

Baltic Sea

IRELAND

DENMARK

ENGLAND

RUSSIAN PRINCIPALITIES

London •

Bremen • • Hamburg

Cologne •

• Kiev

• Paris • Trier

• Ratisbon

FRANCE

Magyars

• Bordeaux

Black Sea

• Ravenna

Barcelona •

ITALY

• Rome

Constantinople •

• Cordova

• Naples

*Mediterranean
Sea*

Moslems

bold seafaring men, hardy and unafraid. Their boats were painted black and had prows carved with figures of sea monsters or dragons. They sailed the northern seas and went farther westward toward the setting sun than any sailors had ever gone. They discovered Iceland and Greenland, and at last under their chief, who was named Leif Ericson, they reached the shores of America. So about the same year that the Christians in Europe were expecting the end of the world—the year 1000—the Vikings had gone to what they thought was "the end of the world."

They called the new country Vineland or Wineland, because they found grapes, from which wine is made, growing there. They did not go far on shore, however, and they thought this new land was only another small island. They had no idea it was a new world. But it was far, far away from their own country, and they soon sailed back home leaving the land for good. The Vikings did nothing more about their discovery, and people forgot all about this new country until nearly five hundred years later.

right: Map showing the routes of the 10th and 11th century Viking explorations

opposite: Lief Ericson landing on the coast of North America

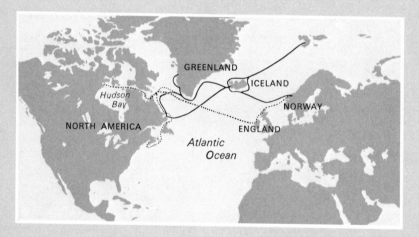

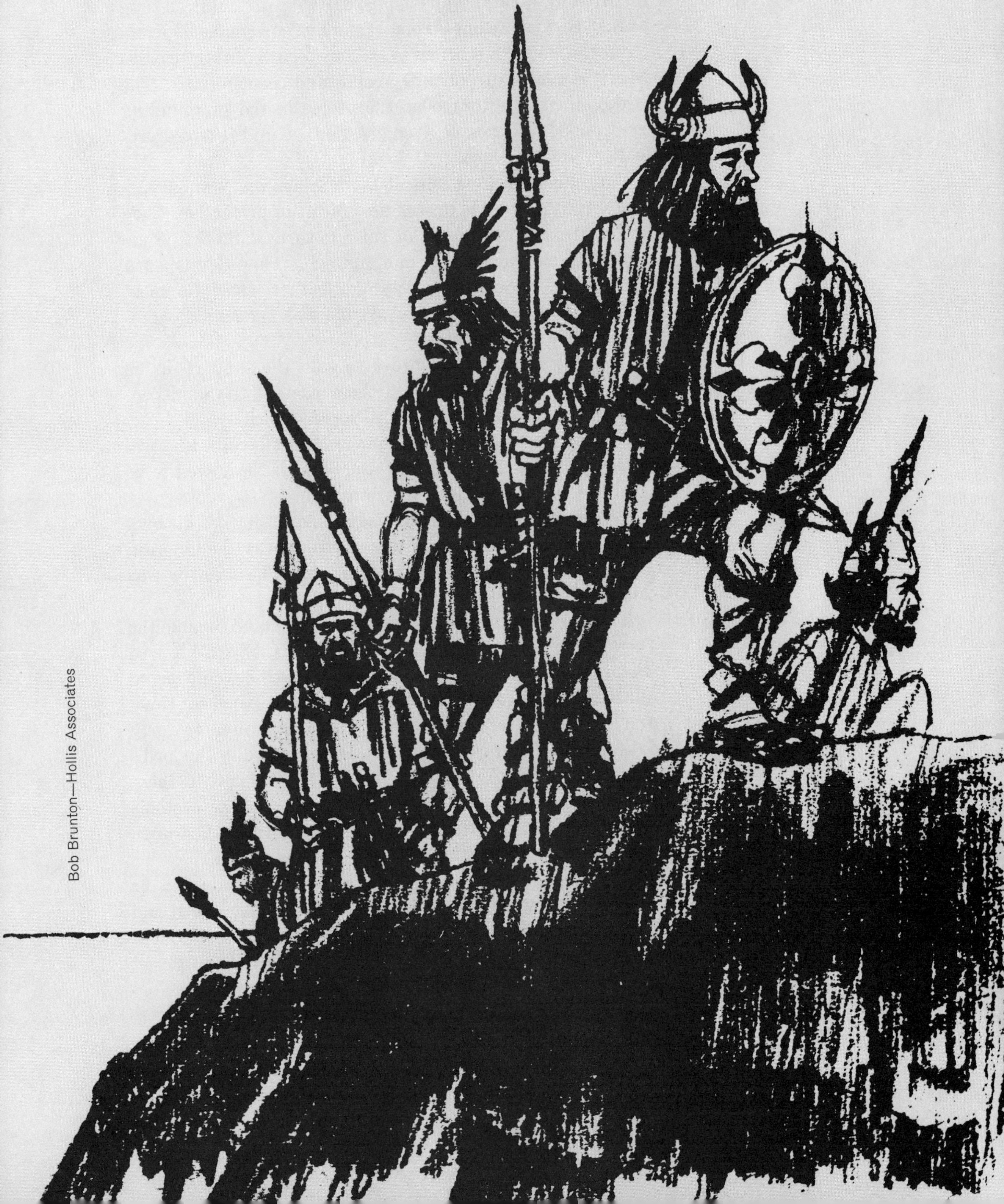

Bob Brunton—Hollis Associates

By the year 1000 there were castles almost everywhere in Europe. These had been built by landowners to protect their property from the many different landgrabbers that invaded Europe. At first these castles were simple buildings fortified by wooden walls supported with dirt. But as time passed, castles became stronger and more permanent. From about the eleventh century to the fourteenth century castles were the center of political, social, and economic life. The lord of the castle controlled the people in the surrounding countryside. The people lived off the land and received protection from the lord.

The raids and invasions of the Vikings and the barbarians forced the people to seek new forms of protection. They had no strong government or ruler to turn to. So the people turned to a local strong man for help. They developed a new way of governing, a way of life that lasted for most of the Middle Ages. This new system was known as *feudalism*. This is how it worked.

The king or prince, in order to gain the support of his generals or warriors, offered them part of the land conquered. Landowners were called lords or nobles.

Each of these landowning lords or nobles became a *vassal* of the man who gave him the land; that is, he vowed to be loyal to him in exchange for protection.

It often happened that this vassal had to pay off his own followers with land. He did this the same way the king did and his followers made promises to him. The receiver was called a *sub-vassal*.

A vassal or a sub-vassal in accepting the land became the "man" of his overlord. He promised to fight with his lord whenever he was needed. This meant that he would bring himself and his troops to battle at his own expense. However, the length of service was generally limited to forty days a year. The vassal also promised to serve in the lord's court. For although there was no law as we know it, there was a definite standard set by the lord and the customs and traditions of the area. One vassal could be called upon to judge the guilt or innocence of a fellow vassal.

Vassals were also responsible for paying certain fees or "aids." These were limited but often heavy. The vassal had to pay something when the eldest son of his lord became a knight, when his eldest daughter married, and when ransom was demanded for the lord if he were captured.

At first the land of the vassal did not necessarily pass from father to son. But this did eventually happen. Thus we

International Visual Aids Center, Belgium

A vassal kneels before
his lord to do homage

find an inheritance tax called *relief* charged when the son
inherited his father's holdings. This varied but it could be
as high as one year's revenue from the land.

Vassals also were required to offer hospitality to the lord
and his party. This included food, shelter, and entertain-
ment. And as the noblemen of the time often traveled with
their own small army for protection, this could be, and
often was, a heavy burden for the average vassal.

Promises of a vassal were made with great ceremony in
a formal setting. This made everything seem more solemn
and binding. The vassal would kneel in front of his lord
with his head uncovered as a sign of respect. He would place
his folded hands between the hands of the lord, and solemnly
promise to observe all his commitments to his lord. This act
was called "doing homage." And once a year, from that time
on, he had to make the same promise over again.

The lord accepted and acknowledged this act of homage
with a kiss. Then he would give his vassal something—a
lance or a glove or even a piece of wood. This gift meant
that the vassal now had the right to use and rule the land
he had received.

This exchange of promises for land was part of a political system unique to the Middle Ages. It substituted for the lack of government. This system was known as *feudalism*. The feudal system was first a political and military organization. The lord promised all who accepted his land and his rule his protection from their enemies. He also promised his vassals that he would not build on or use the land he had given without his vassal's consent. Justice at the court of the lord and respect for the vassal's family were also promised by the lord.

Feudalism was a very personal arrangement between two parties. It was based on two people's promises to guarantee and to do certain things.

Often a castle was built on the piece of land that was given to an important or powerful lord with many sub-vassals and dependent people. There he lived like a little king with all his workers about him. The castle was more than a home. It was also a fort built to protect him from an enemy who might try to take his land and home away by force. A castle, therefore, usually was placed on the top of a hill or on a cliff, so that the enemy could not reach it easily, if at all. These buildings were always surrounded by walls of some type. By the thirteenth century these walls were made of stone and were often ten feet or more thick. Surrounding the walls of most castles was a ditch filled with water called a *moat*. This made it even more difficult for an enemy to get into a castle.

In time of peace the men living under the protection of the castle farmed the land outside of the walls. But when there was a war between lords all the people went inside the castle walls. They carried all the food and cattle and everything else they had so that they could live there for months or even years while the fighting was going on. A castle, therefore, had to be very large to hold so many people and animals for so long a time.

Inside the walls of the castle were many smaller buildings. These housed the people and animals. Other buildings or sections of the castle were built to store food and to make the things needed to run the castle. There might even be a church or a chapel inside the walls. The most important building was, of course, the house of the lord himself; and this was called the *keep*.

At this time the only source of heat was a wood-burning fireplace. This was normally placed in the main room of the house—the hall. This room was like a giant living room and dining room combined. Here meals were served at tables which were simply long, wide boards placed on supports to hold them off the ground. These boards were taken down and put away after the meal was over. This is where we get the names "boarding" and "boardinghouse."

Manners were quite different during the feudal period—especially table manners. Meat was cut with daggers. Some foods were served on plates. Others were served on slices of bread that would soak up gravy. Afterwards the bread would either be thrown to the dogs who roamed around looking for scraps, or it was collected in a basket and given to the poor. There were no forks and spoons until later. Most people ate with their fingers, which they later cleaned by licking them or by wiping them on their clothes. Table manners were more like stable manners. At the end of the meal, a large bowl of water and towels were brought in so that those who wished might wash their hands.

After dinner the household was entertained with songs and stories told by men called minstrels. These men were always welcome. They played and sang and amused the company with true and fanciful tales of the adventures of Charlemagne, King Arthur, and many others.

It seemed that the lord and his people within the castle walls would be absolutely safe from enemy attacks. In the first place, any enemy would have to cross the moat or ditch which surrounded the castle. Across this moat was a drawbridge leading to the entrance or gate of the castle. Over the entrance itself was an iron gate called a *portcullis*, which was usually raised like a window to allow people to pass in and out. But in time of war the drawbridge was raised. In case an enemy was seen approaching and there was no time to raise the drawbridge, this portcullis could be dropped at a moment's notice. With the drawbridge up, there was no way of getting into the castle except by crossing the moat filled with water. Anyone trying to do this would have had stones or melted tar thrown down on him. Instead of windows in the walls of the castle there were only long slits through which the fighters could shoot arrows at the enemy. At the same time, it was very difficult for anyone on the outside to hit the small crack-like opening with arrows.

And yet attacks *were* made on castles. Sometimes the enemy built a tall wooden tower on wheels. They would roll this up as closely as they could get to the walls, and from its top shoot directly over into the castle.

Illustrations on pages 62 and 63
courtesy of International Visiual Aids
Center, Belgium

clockwise from above:

Stealthy armored warriors prepare to attack
under cover of darkness

In times of attack the heavy iron portcullis was
dropped and the drawbridge was raised; the
people stayed inside the thick walls of the castle.

Fierce battles occurred when a castle was
under seige

A lookout was posted to watch for possible attack

This feudal castle was protected by its
hilltop location

Minstrel entertains the ladies of the castle

A defensive moat surrounds the Castle of Ghent

To the serfs fell the rigorous task of repairing
and maintaining the castle

Missiles were hurled from a catapult

Sometimes they built tunnels from the outside—under the ground, under the moat, and under the castle walls into the castle itself. Sometimes they built huge machines called battering rams, and with these they battered down the walls. Sometimes they used machines like great slingshots to throw stones over the walls.

We have talked about the lords and the nobility. They made up one group. The other important group was the clergy—priests, bishops, and abbots. These two groups held most of the land during the Middle Ages.

But the third and last group was by far the largest. These were the commoners—peasants, or *serfs*. Some records say that about eighty-five percent of the people in the Middle Ages were in this last group.

Here is an easy way to remember the classes of the people who lived during this time. There were those who prayed—the clergy; those who fought—the nobility, and those who worked—the peasants.

In time of peace, most of these peasants lived outside the castle walls on the land called the *manor*. Their life centered around the lord's manor. The lord gave them protection and in exchange they gave the lord their labor.

The lords' manors usually were arranged in the same way all over Europe. Each would have a castle, fields, pasture land, a mill or bakehouse, woods, homes for peasants, and a church or chapel. In other words, a medieval manor would have enough things so that almost everything needed could be grown or made.

All these things were owned by the lord of the castle. The peasants only worked this land. To get workers the lord gave small pieces of land to each peasant family on his manor. He kept the largest piece for himself. This was called the lord's domain. This section was worked by the peasants, as part of their payment for their small plots. The rest of the rental of the land was paid by giving the lord a certain part of their own harvest and other services.

The peasants were not like modern renters. They were bound to the land. They could not leave without the lord's permission. If the lord sold or lost his land, the peasants automatically went with it to the new owner. Yet they were not bought or sold and they were not considered slaves, although they were often treated that way and their rights were ignored.

The life of the peasants was hard. All their work and tools were crude and rough. Most of the day they had to use their bare hands and strength to plant, plow, reap, and work the lord's land and their own. They received in return only a little of what they raised. The lord received the rest.

Peasants lived in small, wooden, one-room huts. These huts had dirt floors and thatched roofs. Above the single room there was sometimes a loft reached by a ladder. There was no glass in the windows, which were stuffed with straw in the winter. There was very little in the room except the fireplace and a straw bed. Whole families slept together, in the same clothes they wore during the day. Their food was very poor. Little or no meat was eaten by a peasant family, for they were forbidden by law to hunt or fish on the lord's manor. To break this law might cost them a hand! It is not surprising that peasants usually lived only thirty years or so. These workers were also called serfs. Sometimes a serf who could stand this life no longer ran away. If he was not caught within a year and a day, he was a free man. But if he was caught before the time was up, he had to return to the lord's manor. He was usually punished severely for running away—whipped or branded—because the lords didn't want others to do the same.

65   *(text continued on page 80)*

Street scenes in times of peace showing different kinds of work, China

opposite: Charlemagne, Emperor of the
Holy Roman Empire

below: Even a minor incident could
provoke battle between Northmen who
looked upon fighting as sport

right:
German shield of the
Middle Ages

———————

below: Crossbow
of the Middle Ages

left: Musical score with staff and notes from a 14th century manuscript

above: The lute was a commonly used stringed instrument during medieval times

right: Ornate chalice like those used in the Middle Ages

below: Beautiful glassware made by the Franks

opposite: Beautiful stained-glass window of Chartres Cathedral

right: A Turk in his elegant robes painted by Rembrandt

―――――――

far right: Moslems charge into battle

National Gallery of Art, Washington, D.C.

Bob Brunton—Hollis Associates

left: Medieval painting
of boy with games

below: Guildsmen
working on a building

right: Tapestry woven
in the Near East during
the Middle Ages

opposite top: Siege of a medieval town

opposite bottom: Sacking of a medieval town

left: Siege towers enabled attacking soldiers to get over fortified walls

Knights and the Days of Chivalry

(text continued from page 65)

above: Armored knight
on horseback

During the early feudal period, lords were rough, crude, and uneducated warriors. But as time passed they began to think of themselves as special. They were convinced that their blood made them, and their children, better than common people. The lords began to develop better habits and follow a code of honor. This period is called the "days of chivalry"—which means the time of ladies and gentlemen, not the peasants!

During this time the sons of a lord of a castle were taught how to fight, and how to become knights. Reading and writing were thought to be of no importance. Usually it was considered a waste of time to learn such things unless one were going to be a priest.

Still the training was long for those who had to learn the rules of chivalry. For no one became a knight automatically; this honor had to be earned.

A lord's son stayed with his mother until he was seven years old. Then he went away to begin his training in another castle. For the next seven years he was a page. During this time his chief business was to wait on the ladies of the castle. He ran their errands, carried their messages, and waited on table. He also learned to sing and dance, ride a horse, and to be brave and courteous. It was not unusual for a knight to speak more than one language, but it wasn't until later that some pages learned to read and write.

At fourteen a page became a squire. During this time he waited on the men as he had waited on the ladies when he was a page. He went everywhere with his lord—hunting, fishing, inspecting the lands and shops. He attended to the men's horses and kept the equipment polished and sharp. As a squire, he went to tournaments and battles. Here he led an extra horse, and carried another spear or lance, in case these should be needed.

When he was about twenty-one years old, if he had been a good squire and had learned the lessons he was taught, he became a knight. It was an important step for the boy when he was knighted. He was now ready to take up the business of a man.

In preparation for the ceremony he fasted all day. Then he bathed. This was a sign that he was free from misdeeds, he was good. He dressed in special clothes; a white shirt for purity and a red tunic meaning he was ready to shed blood to uphold his faith and code of honor. Washed and dressed, he prayed all night in the castle church. When day came he appeared before all the guests at the ceremony. Here he solemnly swore always to do these things:

To honor all knights

To be brave and good

To fight for the Christian religion

To protect the weak

To honor women

To love God

These were his vows. A white leather belt was then put on him and gold spurs were fastened on his boots. Then he knelt, and his lord and teacher struck him over the shoulders with the flat side of a sword, saying as he did so, "I dub thee Knight" and the new knight responded, "I pledge my life and allegiance to God and to my lord." Forever after he would be called Sir.

A knight went into battle covered with a suit of armor made of iron rings or steel plates like fish scales, and with a helmet or hood of iron. This suit protected him from the arrows and lances of the enemy. He carried a shield, a sword, and an eight-foot lance; these were the weapons of war used during this time.

Knights were so completely covered by their armor that when sides became mixed up in fighting, they could not tell one another apart. It was impossible to know which were enemies.

So the knights wore a design on the outside of the coat that went over their armor. This design might be a lion, a rose, or some other ornament and was known as a *coat of arms*.

A knight, as we said, was first of all taught to be a gentleman, and we still speak of one who has good manners and is courteous, especially to ladies, as knightly or chivalrous. When a knight came into the presence of a lady, he took off his helmet. It meant, "You are my friend, and so I do not need my helmet." That is why gentlemen raise their hats nowadays when they meet ladies.

But the most important thing the knights had to learn was to fight. For during the feudal days, war was common. They were not big wars like the Greek or Roman wars. Most of them were private fights between an overlord and his vassal or between two rival lords. Land was wealth and there were few ways to get more land. The main way a man could get more land was to win it in a war.

These armored knights did not fear fighting. They would charge straight at each other, fighting hand to hand with their swords and battle axes. To the winner went the honor, the plunder, and the prisoners.

Does it seem strange that they would want prisoners? The way the feudal rule was established, prisoners were held for ransom. When they were captured, knights, peasants, and vassals had to pay for their release.

The knights' love of war made things harder for the peasants. Their fields were destroyed, crops ruined, cattle killed, and villages and woods burned to the ground. Finally the church stepped in and tried to get the knights to obey a rule called the "Truce of God." This started about 1025 in France. It forbade fighting on certain days. At first it was only Friday, Saturday, and Sunday. It was later lengthened to cover from sunset on Wednesday to sunrise on Monday and all of Lent, or other religious seasons. Another rule

opposite: The lion on this coat of arms symbolizes courage

above: A knight with his coat of arms

right: Lords and their vassals engaged in almost constant warfare. A variety of weapons was used. In the foreground is a club used for breaking armor called a mace.

below: A lone survivor views the bodies of his comrades

called the "Peace of God" said the Church would excommunicate, or exclude, anyone who fought or killed people who were clergy, those who were being peaceful, and anyone who damaged church property.

Each country and each age has had its own games or sports in which it took special delight. The Greeks had Olympic Games. The Romans had chariot races and gladiatorial contests. But the chief sport of the knights was a kind of sham battle called a tournament, or tourney.

The tournament was held in a field known as the *lists*. Large crowds with banners flying and trumpets blowing would gather around the lists to watch these sham fights. The knights on horseback took their places at opposite ends of the lists. They carried lances and swords, the points of which were covered so that they would not make a wound. At a given signal, they rushed toward the center of the field and tried with their lances to throw each other off their horses. This was called *jousting*. The knight who succeeded in throwing the other knight was the winner and was presented with a ribbon or a keepsake by one of the ladies. He also received the horse and armor of his beaten opponent.

Knights were fond of hunting with dogs. But they also hunted with a trained falcon, or hawk. Both lords and ladies delighted in this sport. The falcon was trained to catch other birds, such as wild ducks and pigeons, and also small animals. The falcon was chained to the wrist of the lord or lady, and its head was covered with a hood as it was carried out to hunt. When a bird was seen the hood was removed, and the falcon, which was very swift, was released to swoop upon its prey and capture it. Thereupon the hunter would come up, take the captured animal, and replace the hood on the falcon.

Hunting wild boar, which is a kind of pig with sharp tusks, was popular, too. This was more dangerous and therefore supposed to be more of a man's sport.

Falcons were used in hunting

opposite top: Horsemen use lances as they joust in a tournament

opposite bottom: Hunting wild boar

A Pirate's Great Grandson

When Alfred was king, the Northmen, called Danes, had raided England. At the same time their cousins the Norsemen had raided the coast of France.

King Alfred at last had to give the Danes a part of the English coast, and they settled down and became Christians.

The French king, Charles the Simple, did the same thing in 912. In order to save himself from further raids, the Norsemen were given a part of the French coast. Then, as their cousins had done, they settled down and became Christians.

These Norsemen who raided France were led by a bold and brave pirate named Rollo. Rollo was married to the daughter of Charles. In return for this gift of land, Rollo became a Christian and was baptized Robert. He became the first duke of Normandy and vassal to the king of France.

That part of France which was given the Norsemen is still called Normandy today. The people were known as Normans.

In 1066 a very powerful duke ruled over Normandy. His name was William. He was the cousin of the English king, Edward the Confessor.

William, was strong in will, and strong in rule over his people. He could shoot an arrow farther, straighter, and with more deadly effect than any of his knights. No one else was strong enough even to bend the bow he used.

William was only a duke, not a king. He was also a vassal of the king of France. He wanted to be king of England, which was just across the English Channel from Normandy.

It so happened that a young English nobleman named Harold was shipwrecked on the coast of Normandy about 1064. He was found and brought before William. It seemed likely that someday Harold would be king of England, and William thought this would be a good chance to get England for himself. So before he would let Harold leave, he made the young man promise that when his turn came to be king he would give him England—just as if that country were a house or a suit of armor that could be given away! Then

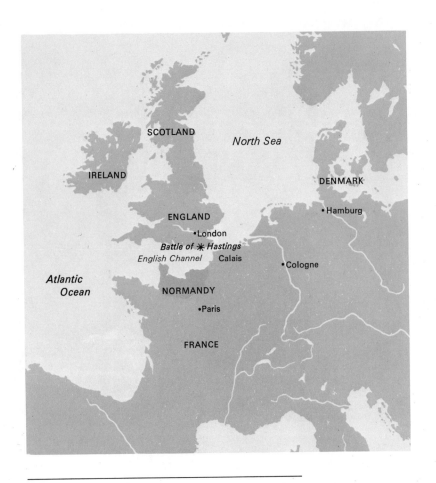

Bob Brunton—Hollis Associates

in order that this promise should be solemnly binding, William made Harold place his hand on the altar and swear, just as people place a hand on the Bible now when they take an oath. After Harold had sworn on the altar, William had the top lifted and showed Harold that below it were the bones of some of the Christian saints. Swearing on the bones of a saint was the most solemn kind of oath one could possibly take. It was thought one would not dare to break such an oath for fear of the wrath of God.

Then Harold returned to England and at last was chosen king. The Saxon people naturally would not let him give England to William. Besides, Harold said that such an oath, which had been taken against his will, an oath which had been forced on him by a trick, was not binding.

When William heard that Harold had been made king, he was very angry. He said that he had been cheated and that Harold had broken his oath.

above left: Map showing Normandy

above right: Norman soldiers had better weapons and armor than the Teutons

above left: Portrait of William the Conqueror

above right: Harold was crowned king in 1066

At once William began to assemble his army. Some records say he had about 2,000 knights and 3,000 squires and archers, all of whom he had to carry across the channel by boat. To do this, William got together a fleet of ships. These were small vessels holding about a dozen horses plus men.

At this time Harold had been fighting the Danes in the north. Hearing of the invasion, he turned south to meet the new enemy. Harold took a strong position on a hill at Hastings.

The English fought furiously on foot with spears and axes to defend themselves against the Norman knights who attacked their line. Indeed, they had almost won the battle when William gave an order to his men to pretend they were running away. The English then followed, wildly rejoicing, and running after the Normans. Just as soon as the English were scattered and in disorder, however, William gave another signal, and his horsemen turned around and rode down upon the pursuing English soldiers. The English were taken by surprise, and before they could get into fighting units again, they were cut down and defeated. Harold, their king, and a band of his picked troops fought till evening when all were killed, including Harold. This was the Battle of Hastings which occurred in 1066. It is one of the most famous battles in English history.

William divided England among his nobles as if it were a pie. This was the feudal way. In accepting the land, the knights promised to fight for him and do as he said. William, a clever ruler, made sure that none of his Norman followers held more land than he did. Later he gathered all the landholders together on the plain of Salisbury and he made them take a solemn oath never to fight against him. Now these nobles might have gotten together and fought him except for one other thing. William had an army of "freemen" loyal only to him. He kept this force to make sure the nobles never broke their promises.

William was a splendid boss and very businesslike. He set to work to organize his government. He had a list made of all the people in England and all the property they owned. This giant record was called the *Domesday Book*. From this book William could make sure he got all the money and goods that were owed to him and that no one would cheat him.

In order that no mischief might take place at night, William started what was called the *curfew*. Every evening at a certain hour, a bell was rung. Then all lights had to be put out, and everyone had to go indoors.

One thing that William did made the English very angry. He was extremely fond of hunting, but there was no good place where he could hunt near London. So in order to have a place for hunting, he destroyed a large number of village houses and farms and turned that part of the country into a forest. This was called the New Forest, and though it is now about nine hundred years *old* it is still called New to this day.

On the whole, William gave England a good government and made it a much safer and better place in which to live than it had been under its former rulers.

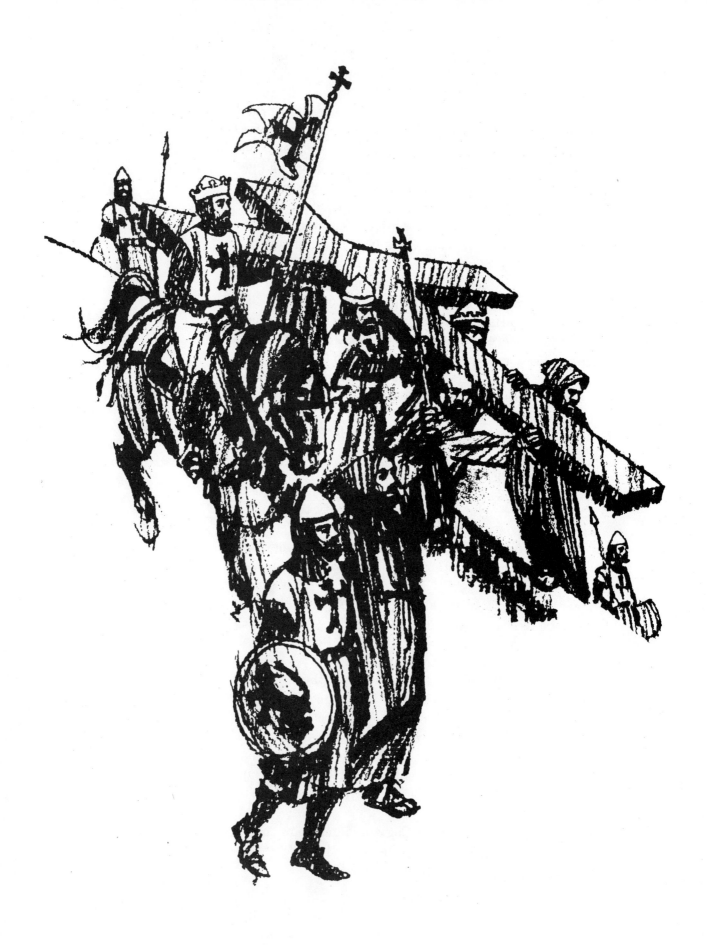

A Great Adventure:
The Crusades

In the Dark Ages Christians everywhere in Europe went to Jerusalem if they could. They wanted to see the actual spot where Christ had been crucified and they wanted to pray at the Holy Sepulcher.

It took them months and sometimes years to reach Jerusalem. These travelers were called *pilgrims*, and their trip was called a pilgrimage. Records say that 11,000 people took this pilgrimage in 1065 under the leadership of a German bishop.

Now during the eleventh century Jerusalem belonged to Seljuk (sell-jook') Turks, who were Moslems. They held almost all of Asia Minor. They defeated the army of the emperor of Constantinople, and even began to threaten the safety of the city itself.

The crusaders march to battle in Jerusalem

These Turks did not like the Christian pilgrims, and did not treat them very well. Indeed, on their return some of the pilgrims told frightful stories of the way they had been treated by the Turks and the way the holy places in Jerusalem were also treated.

At this time there was a pope in Rome named Urban II. He was the head of all the Christians in the world. Urban heard these tales that the pilgrims told. He also heard the pleas for help from the emperor at Constantinople. It was a terrible thing for the Holy City, as Jerusalem was called, and the Holy Land, where the city was located, to be ruled by Moslems instead of Christians. So Urban made a great speech at Clermont in France. He urged all good Christians to stop fighting each other and to begin to fight for the faith. His speech was so good that when he was finished, as the story goes, the large crowd cried out together, "God wills it." The military pilgrimage to Jerusalem to fight the Turks had began.

Peter the Hermit inspired the people to save the Holy Land

There lived at that time a monk whom people called Peter the Hermit. Peter had made a pilgrimage to Jerusalem and was very angry at what he saw there. So he, too, began to tell people everywhere that they ought to fight to save Jerusalem. He rode about on a mule and talked to people in the churches, on the street corners, and in the market places. He was such a wonderful orator that those who heard him wept at his descriptions and begged to go with him.

Before long, thousands upon thousands of people, old and young, men and women, and even some children had pledged themselves to join a band to go to Jerusalem and take it away from the Moslems.

Because Christ had died on the cross, the sign of the Christians was the cross. The pilgrims adopted this sign. They cut pieces of red cloth in the form of a cross and sewed them on their right shoulders. This meant they were willing to die for their faith as soldiers of the cross. A word was developed from the Latin word for cross—crux. The new word was *crusader* and it meant all those who fought for the cross.

But not all went just for the love of their God. Some went in search of plunder from the East. Others because they sought to absolve themselves from all past misdeeds by this one good act. Still others, debtors and criminals, joined the crusades because the pope had promised to pardon them. And to all who might fall in battle the pope promised immediate entry into heaven. This was very much like the promise to Moslems who died for their beliefs.

The plan was to start in the summer of 1096 but a great many were so anxious to get started that they didn't wait. Led by Peter the Hermit and another pious man, a poor knight named Walter the Penniless, a large group, mostly peasants, started off for Jerusalem.

They had no idea how far they would have to travel. They had no idea how long it would take, no idea how they would get food to eat on their journey, no idea where they would sleep. They simply trusted in Peter the Hermit and believed that the Lord would provide everything and show them the way.

Onward they marched, thousands upon thousands, toward the East and far-off Jerusalem. Thousands upon thousands of them died from disease and from hunger on the way. Finally the crusaders reached the city of Constantinople. Disaster struck, for the Turks had heard of their coming. They attacked this poor disorganized group and killed almost all of them. This ill-fated crusade was called the *Peasant's Crusade.*

Meanwhile the crusaders forming the main army were getting ready to march. Led by great noble knights they began the long journey to Constantinople. From here they sailed across the Bosporus to the coast of Asia Minor. The Turks attacked this brave band, too, but were defeated. The crusaders kept moving toward Jerusalem. Finally in 1099, after nearly four years and much suffering and hardship and death, the band of survivors reached the walls of the Holy City. When at last they saw Jerusalem before them, they went wild with joy. They fell on their knees and wept and prayed. They sang hymns and thanked God for bringing them to the end of their journey. Then they attacked! So fierce was the combat that the Christians overcame the walled city within five weeks. They entered the gates and killed so many thousands that it is said the streets of the Holy City ran with blood. Killing and looting were widespread, each crusader seeking to profit from this conquest. This was the way of feudal warfare and conquest as it had come from the days of the barbarians.

Peasants who made up the First Crusade

After praying at the Holy Sepulcher and thus fulfilling their vows, most of the crusaders returned home. They left behind one of their leaders, Godfrey. He was appointed ruler of the city. He was not called king, but "Baron and Defender of the Holy Sepulcher." In all, the conquered

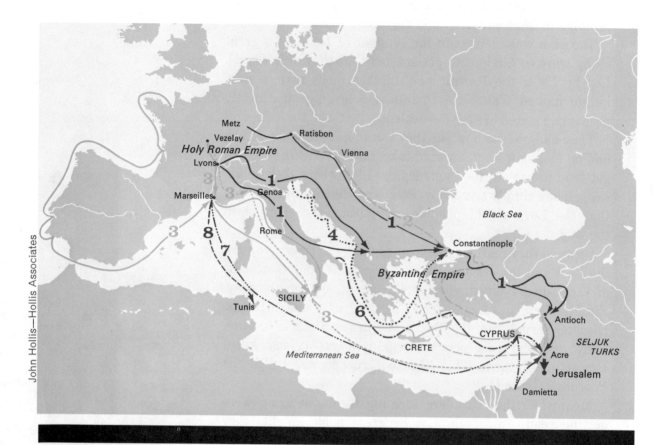

Metz
Vezelay
Ratisbon
Holy Roman Empire
Vienna
Lyons
3
1
Genoa
1
Marseilles
3
Black Sea
Rome
3
8
4
1
2
7
Constantinople
Byzantine Empire
Tunis
SICILY
6
1
3
Antioch
CYPRUS
CRETE
Acre
SELJUK TURKS
Mediterranean Sea
Jerusalem
Damietta

territory was organized into four areas or states. These were ruled in the feudal manner.

Jerusalem was now ruled by Christians. A new type of monk helped rule the city. They were all knights but they also bound themselves to the three vows of monkhood—poverty, chastity, and obedience. These warrior monks were called the Knights of the Temple and the Knights of St. John, or Hospitalers. They protected the holy places from attack, aided and protected pilgrims, and cared for the sick and needy.

Within a short time, however, Jerusalem again was in the hands of the Moslems. So the Christians in the West started a second crusade. Then during the next two hundred years there was one crusade after another—eight or nine in all. Sometimes these later crusades won back Jerusalem for a short while, but most of them were not successful.

The third crusade took place about a hundred years after the first. This has been called the *Crusade of Romance*, mostly because of the high positions and romantic qualities of its three leaders. There were three kings leading the army—Richard of England, Philip Augustus of France, and Frederick Barbarossa of Germany. They all started on this venture, but they didn't all finish it.

Only King Richard finished. Many think it would have been better if he had gone home instead of staying to run the crusade. But Richard thought going on a crusade was more fun than governing England. In fact, from his record, one might say he thought any place was better than England. In the ten years of his reign, Richard spent only about a year there. He was always somewhere else. Although he had his faults, Richard was the kind of man that men and women love. He was kind and gentle, yet strong and brave. So he was called Richard the Lionhearted. People loved him, but they feared him too, for he punished severely and justly all those who misbehaved.

Even Richard's enemies admired him. The Moslem general who had conquered the Holy City in 1187 was a man named Saladin. He, unlike the other Moslem generals, allowed the Christians to leave with their property. He did this, as it was later reported, to show the Christians how good was the religion of Mohammed.

When Richard and Saladin faced each other, the fighting began and went on and on. Neither side was able to win a complete victory. Finally after much bloodshed, a truce

Historical Pictures Service, Chicago

opposite top: Routes of the Crusades

opposite bottom: Knight leaving a castle for the Second Crusade

above: Saladin in the midst of battle

was arranged in 1192. This truce or agreement said that the Moslems could rule Jerusalem but they promised to treat the pilgrims and the Holy Sepulcher with great respect and allow pilgrims to continue to visit the Holy City. And so ended the third crusade. Richard left the East and returned home.

On his way home, Richard, who was traveling in disguise, was captured by one of his enemies—the archduke of Austria. He was put in prison and held for a large ransom.

Richard's coat of arms was a design of three lions, one above the other; and this same design of three lions now forms part of the shield of England.

After Richard's crusade there was a fourth crusade that failed miserably. Then in the year 1212 there was a crusade of children only. This was known therefore as the *Children's Crusade*. It was led by a twelve-year-old French boy named Stephen.

Children from all over France and Germany believed the fourth crusade failed because of a lack of faith. They left their homes and their families and marched south to the Mediterranean Sea. Here they expected the waters of the sea would part and allow them to march on dry land to Jerusalem. They had read in the Bible that the waters of the Red Sea had separated to allow the Israelites to leave Egypt. But the Mediterranean did not part.

Some sailors, however, offered to take the children to Jerusalem in their ships. They said they would do it for nothing, just for the love of the Lord. But these sailors were pirates, and as soon as they got the children on board their ships they steered them straight across the Mediterranean to Africa into the very land of their enemies, the Moslems. Here, it is said, the pirates sold the children as slaves. Few if any were ever seen again.

The last two crusades were led by a king of France called Louis IX in 1248 and 1270. He was so pious and so devoted to the Lord that he was made a saint. So in the Catholic Church this king is known as St. Louis. Yet the efforts of this holy man failed as the others had. So by the end of the thirteenth century, the crusaders were home for good. Jerusalem and all land in the Near East and North Africa were still in the hands of the Moslems.

The crusades did not succeed in their objective, which was to keep Jerusalem for the Christians. Yet in spite of that, they did a great deal of good. When the crusades first started, the crusaders were not nearly as civilized as the people they went to conquer. But travel sometimes teaches people more than books, and it taught the crusaders. They learned the customs of the Greeks and Moslems, their languages and literature, history and art. So the crusades did for learning what schools would have done if they had existed. They taught the people many things and started the renewal of education in the West, which eventually ended the Dark Ages. They learned about gunpowder from the Moslems who had learned about it from the Chinese. The crusaders also learned about guns, though the first gun was a very, very simple affair. Within a short time these two discoveries changed the world. Each contributed to the downfall of feudalism and the end of the armored knight.

The crusaders returned with a taste for many of the luxuries of life they had found in the East. These fineries included spices, carpets, velvets, silk, sugar, drugs, and jewels. To meet this demand traders began regular trips to the East. The increased flow of goods brought prosperity to the West. This brought into being a new class or group of people—the middle class or the townspeople.

Another thing happened because of these crusades. During the course of the two hundred years of fighting a great many noblemen were killed. Those who survived were away from their manors for great lengths of time. When they returned they discovered that, in their absence, many things had changed at home. The kings had used this time to their advantage. They had begun the long process of bringing all the people under the king's law and the king's power.

Towns of the Middle Ages

During and after the crusades cities began to grow. Some were left from the Roman founders, such as Lyons, Marseilles, Cologne, London, and Cordova, which were once garrison towns.

New towns developed around fortresses, monasteries, and castles. Here people could be protected. Usually these cities belonged to the local lord, as did the land worked by the serfs. Since the lords were more interested in their farm holdings than they were in the cities, the cities usually had more freedom. Serfs fled to cities, because if they lived free and undiscovered for a year and a day, they were truly free. Their lord could not make them return to the castle-manor.

Cities grew in many ways. As travel became safer and trade grew, towns along trade roads, rivers, or seaports became larger.

Like a castle, the medieval city was protected by a strong defensive wall and often a moat. A gate guarded the entrance to the city; this was closed at night and guarded.

below: Peasant plowing outside the walls of a fortified town

The cities of the Middle Ages often had the same general plan. Each had an open space in the center of the town that was called by many different names—square, place, piazza. Around this open area were built the great cathedrals and other important buildings. Cathedrals were like meeting houses. Money, time, and labor were given generously by the people for their cathedral. Some cathedrals were so well built they are still used today. In the square were set up the stalls from which the merchants and tradesmen sold their merchandise. People gathered here to socialize after church services, to view a play, or to watch games of sport.

Streets led from the square to other parts of the town or city. These were built only for walking. Wagons used only the wider main streets. Side streets were just wide enough for a horseman carrying a lance across his saddle to pass. The crowded buildings that lined the streets were protected from heat and cold. Generally these streets were not paved, for this practice did not become common until the late Middle Ages.

Buildings in the town were often six or seven stories above the ground. Space was scarce, for most people wanted to live inside the protection of the wall that surrounded the town. This is why the old first sections of cities often were crowded. This was the case of the old London Bridge, on which were built homes and stores. Houses or buildings tended to lean out over the street. This leaning increased with each story so that it was often possible for a person living on the top story to reach out and touch the top part of the building across the street.

Walking down the streets during the Middle Ages was often a hazardous proposition. Refuse and garbage of all kinds were simply thrown out of the windows. It is believed that the courteous gesture of having the man walk on the outside when accompanying a woman came during this time. By so doing he would protect his partner from being dashed with refuse from above.

The lack of sanitation and water systems often caused plagues and fevers to rage through a town. Fire was another problem, for most of the buildings of this period were of wood.

The renewed interest in trade and commerce in Europe brought about the building and growth of many towns and cities. But outside the town, travel was difficult. Most of the trade was begun by peddlers who traveled from place to place and attended many local fairs and markets. The

roads were not at all like those the Romans had built. Nearly all the Roman roads had fallen into ruin. Dirt roads of this time were full of ruts and holes. In rainy weather and in winter they became muddy, swampy traps. The nobles and wealthy people traveled on horseback. Others traveled on foot or by cart. Crossing streams and rivers sometimes was dangerous. If there was a bridge, it was not always kept in good repair by the local ruler.

All along the roads and travel routes, the lack of law often added to the hazards of a journey. Robbers lurked behind rocks. But robbers were not the only danger. Areas were often ruled by local nobles, rather than the "law of the land." When someone attempted to pass from one area to another, the ruler sometimes demanded a payment of money or goods. This payment was called a *toll*. Tolls had to be paid if a man wanted to cross a noble's land, or use his road or his bridge.

Towns in the Middle Ages were built, in many cases, on land granted by the local noble lord. Towns established in this manner paid a certain fee to the local lord. As the towns grew and became more successful in business, the townspeople found it necessary to make the lord agree to certain things. Generally, the first thing they demanded was more freedom. As long as they were dominated by the lords, they were like serfs and the lord took too much as his share of their profits.

opposite: Narrow streets in a medieval town

above left: Travelers outside of towns were in constant danger of highway robbery

As a result of this growing desire for freedom, there were many revolts in the twelfth century. The townspeople demanded written proof granting them certain rights. These were called *charters*. These, if granted, were the rules that governed the town. More charters were granted to towns during the crusades than had been granted previously; this added to the development of town life.

If a town were free, there was a guard maintained day and night. The guard watched and if there were an approaching attack, he gave warning to the people by ringing a bell.

Some of the most famous towns in the Middle Ages were in Italy. Here trade seems never to have stopped entirely. Genoa, Venice, and other towns maintained trade which was greatly increased during the crusades. Italian businessmen traveled to the Orient and brought back products from the East. These goods were transported to other parts of Europe, particularly to towns in the north. The merchants in the north dealt with Venice. They either carried their goods by land across the mountains and down the river systems or they sent them by sea around Spain, through the English Channel to Flanders.

Businessmen in the medieval world had problems that today's professional men do not have. There was very little money in the Middle Ages. Barter—the trading or exchange of one thing for another—was all right for a manor, but not for a growing business. Money is necessary for large-scale business. Since there were very few gold or silver mines in western Europe, the kings and feudal lords could not produce this metal for their coins. Those coins that were made were of poor quality and irregular in shape.

Businessmen were hampered also by the concept of what was a fair price. A "just price" was considered that which was merely enough to cover the cost of materials and the labor involved.

Businessmen discovered ways to overcome these problems. They formed organizations called guilds, which met various needs.

Men who did the same kind of work belonged to the same guild. There were three major guilds in the Middle Ages. The *religious guilds* were groups of men who joined together for special purposes such as helping the poor and caring for the sick. The *merchant guilds* were tradesmen who joined together and made rules about sales and purchases and set standards for items manufactured. From these

A medieval charter

Novgorod

•Edinburgh

Dublin •

North Sea

Baltic Sea

•Danzig

Bremen •Hamburg

London • •Amsterdam

Ghent •Antwerp

Calais •Cologne

•Leipzig

•Kiev

*Atlantic
Ocean*

Brest •

•Paris

•Krakow

•Vienna

Buda• •Pest

•Trent

•Milan •Venice

•Leon

Genoa •

Marseilles • •Florence

Black Sea

•Lisbon •Madrid

Toledo •Barcelona

•Rome

•Cordova

•Naples

•Constantinople

•Cadiz

*Mediterranean
Sea*

Damascus •

Tripoli •

top: Map of
towns and cities
in the Middle
Ages

below: A master
weaver works at
his loom

guilds came the last type of guild organization, the *craft guild*. All the shoemakers, bakers, candlestick makers, tailors, carpenters, and so on had their own organizations which set up rules. These rules governed the length of time a person should work, wages, prices, and training of the young men in the craft. Guild members punished anyone who did not follow these rules and they stopped anyone from coming into a town to set up business unless he was a member of a guild.

These guilds were very much like modern trade unions. On the small-business level of the time, each member of a guild looked forward to being an owner someday. They were independent workmen working for themselves. It was hundreds of years before the large-scale production of modern times took over this independent production.

If a young man wanted to enter a trade, he had to do certain things. He first became an *apprentice*; that is, he joined a "master" tradesman, paid a fee, and moved into the master's house, which was also his store. It was the custom to have the shop in front and the living quarters of the family in the rear or on the second story of the building. As an apprentice, the young man worked for the master. In exchange for his labor, he received his training, food, clothing, and shelter. After a certain period of time —three to twelve years depending on the craft—he advanced to the next step in his training. He became a *journeyman*. As a journeyman he received wages but was still attached by law to his master. At about the age of twenty-three, the journeyman sought admission into the guild as a *master*. To be accepted he had to prove his ability and his honesty. In later years this usually required a "masterpiece," which was an item made to meet all the specifications of all the other members of the guild. A shoemaker made a pair of shoes, a tailor made a suit of clothes, a baker made loaves of bread, and so on.

This was the way the cities and towns of the Middle Ages were run. These towns were the first step taken during the Middle Ages toward a more advanced society. The people were turning from the land to the arts. The increased use of money and the growth of manufacturing enabled people who were not nobles or knights to better themselves as freemen. This was a new class of people. The kings in the thirteenth and fourteenth centuries were to use this group to further their aims against the nobility.

John, Whom Nobody Loved

Richard the Lion-Hearted, whom everybody loved, had a brother named John, whom nobody loved. John became king, but he turned out to be a very wicked man.

John was afraid that his young nephew, Arthur, might be made king in his place; it is believed that John had Arthur murdered.

John held great amounts of land in France. These he obtained through his Norman ancestors and successful marriages. But King Philip Augustus of France was determined to kick the English out of his country. He wanted to be the highest power in France.

John was a vassal of the king of France. But John broke his contract and married a lady engaged to one of his own vassals. This was against all codes of honor and against the feudal law. Philip Augustus, John's feudal lord, called him to appear at the French court. John refused to come. He also refused to do homage for his land. As a result, the court—following Philip's instructions—took away from John much of the land, including Normandy, Anjou, and Maine, leaving only the southwest corner of France in the hands of the English.

Then John got into a quarrel with the pope in Rome. The pope at that time was Innocent III, the head of all Christians. Pope Innocent III ordered King John to make a certain man bishop in England, but John wouldn't do it. He wanted his own minister to be Archbishop of Canterbury. The pope threatened to close up all the churches in England if John didn't do as he was told. Still John refused. So in 1208 the pope placed England under "interdict." This meant that all the churches in England were closed until John gave in to the pope. The church was the one most important thing in everyone's life during the Middle Ages. Nothing else mattered so much. The closing of the churches meant that no services could be held in any church. It meant that children could not be baptized, and it was believed that unbaptized children, if they died, could not go to heaven. It meant that couples could not be married. It meant that the dead could not be given a Christian burial.

The people of England were shocked. It was as if heaven had put a curse on them. They were afraid that terrible things would happen to them. Of course the people blamed John, for he was the cause of the churches being closed. They were so angry with him that he became afraid of what his people might do to him. John was angry, too. He took church property and began to punish the religious people in England. The pope excommunicated him in 1209. Finally in 1212 the pope declared that the people of England no longer owed allegiance or support to John. He threatened to make another man, Philip of France, king of England. At last, when he saw the army being readied by Philip, John gave in. He agreed to do everything that at first he said he would not do, and more besides. He went so far that he gave England to the pope and received it back as a vassal. But this fight between the church and state was only the beginning of John's mistakes.

John had an idea that the world was made for the king and that people were put on the earth simply so that the king might have servants to work for him, to earn money for him, to do what he wished them to do. Many of the kings in those days felt the same way, though they did not go as far as John did. John ordered people who were rich to give him money. If they refused to give him all he asked, he put them in prison and had them tortured or even put to death.

John demanded more and more, until at last his barons could not stand his actions any longer. They gathered together an army of nobles to march against John. They met him just outside London at Runnymede Meadow on the Thames River. Here they forced John to agree to certain rights of his subjects. These were written down in Latin on the 15th of June in 1215. This list of things the barons made John agree to was called by the Latin name for a great agreement, which is *Magna Carta*.

---

opposite: King John signing the Magna Carta

John publicly accepted this charter and affixed his seal to it. This seal was of a special design used only by King John. He pressed the seal into a piece of hot wax which was dropped on the agreement where one would have signed. When the wax was dried the image was fixed. Special seals are used by governments today.

John agreed in the Magna Carta to give the barons some rights. No taxes beyond the feudal dues could be collected unless the Great Council voted "yes." Without their consent the king could not collect extra taxes. The charter also listed the right of all "freemen" to a fair trial. The king could not put in prison, banish, or punish anyone unless he was judged by his peers or by the law of the land. Peers means those of equal rank. These are two of the most important rights that John agreed to in the Magna Carta.

Kings who came after John were made to agree to the same things. So after 1215, the king in England was supposed to be the servant of the people, instead of the people being servants of the king.

The Magna Carta said that the law is a higher power than a king and a king cannot break a law. The freemen of England in later centuries used the Magna Carta to help them fight kings who were unfair or cruel.

From this small beginning, England's Parliament developed.

The East

The Golden Age in Chinese history began about 618 and ended in 906. While the West, as we have seen, had been beaten and broken by the invasions, the great nation in the Far East had been enjoying and furthering a great cultural civilization. China gave to the East what Greece and Rome had given to the West.

One of her greatest emperors, T'ai Tsung (597–649), was responsible for fighting off border invaders. He kept his territory free and ruled from his capital. Although he followed the teachings of Confucius, he allowed Christian monks and Moslem teachers to preach in his land.

He also furthered the development of trade routes. Rice, silk, spices, and many other treasures were carried by land and sea to India, Egypt, Constantinople, and Greece.

After his death, his family—the T'ang Dynasty—continued to rule in China. And from 713 to 756, China entered a period of great progress in the promotion of culture and learning. This was due not to the emperor who ruled at the time, but to a lady in his court. She was called the Oriental Cleopatra because of the influence she had on important men. Her name was Lady Yang. Because of her, some of China's greatest poets, artists, and scholars had an opportunity to make great contributions to culture; they were rewarded by the court for their work.

During the T'ang rule of China, printing was first developed. Paper had been made in China as early as the first century after Christ. This was in use for all hand-written manuscripts. The Buddhist monks, however, felt that they would be of more help to the people if they could give them copies of the sacred writing. So they worked to make a way of reproducing the writing on a larger scale. Finally they were successful.

The writings were carved on a block of wood. This was covered with ink, and paper was then pressed against the block. When the paper was removed, the image came with it. This was the beginning of printing, although it was hundreds of years before the people in the West learned this art and began to use it.

When the rule of this great family ended, Chinese monarchs were weak. There was no outstanding leader until about 960. Then a family known as Sung came into power. Backed by the army, the first Sung performed a great service to his country by keeping out of China a barbaric tribe in the West. This tribe, known as the Tartars, was a constant threat to the security of the Chinese. When they were unable to defeat the Tartars, the Sungs began the practice of paying off the tribal chiefs. But the Tartar chiefs were greedy. Every year they demanded and received more payment. It is recorded that in 1043 they received more than 200,000 ounces of silver, large amounts of precious silk cloth, and many other goods.

Yet in the end, this payment proved useless. Within 200 years, the Tartars overwhelmed the weak Chinese rulers. This was due mainly to the coming of one of history's most terrifying characters. A giant military warrior—fierce and barbaric—arose during the twelve hundreds. His name was Genghis Khan (1162–1227). A member of the Tartar family, he broke away from the main tribe. He called his group the *Mongols*. He organized them into a terrific military force that swept over the land, conquering almost all of China and Central Asia.

---

opposite: A Chinese wooden sculpture from the thirteenth century

Born and bred to conquer, Genghis Khan and his men destroyed or took over everything and everyone that came before them. They invaded, burned, and destroyed thousands of towns and cities. They killed men, women, and children by the millions.

Genghis Khan conquered the whole land from the Pacific Ocean to the eastern part of Europe. The Mongol Empire stretched all the way across Asia. But at last he stopped. With this kingdom he seemed to be satisfied. And he might well have been, for his empire was larger than the Roman Empire, or even that of Alexander the Great.

Dotted lines show extent of Han Empire
Shaded area shows Mongol Empire at its height

opposite: Genghis Khan, the mighty Mongol warrior

left: The Mongol Empire

When Genghis died, things were no better. His son, who was just as frightful as his father had been, conquered still more country. From China in the East, the Mongol Empire soon stretched all the way across Asia to the Danube River.

But the grandson of Genghis Khan was much less ferocious. His name was Kublai Khan, and he was quite different from his ancestors. His capital in China was called Peking. Kublai Khan's main interest was in building magnificent palaces and surrounding himself with beautiful gardens. He made a wonderful capital for himself.

Far from Peking, in the north of Italy, was a city built on the water. Its streets were of water, and boats were used instead of carriages. This, of course, was Venice. About the year 1300, two brothers named Polo lived there. One of them had a son named Marco who traveled with his father and uncle when they started East looking for trade and adventure. After many years, they at last came to the magnificent palace of Kublai Khan.

They told Kublai Khan all about their own land. They also told him of the Christian religion and many other things he had never heard about.

The emperor was so much interested in the Polos and in the stories they told, that he persuaded them to stay with him. He gave them rich presents and made them advisers and assistants in ruling his empire. So the Polos learned the language and stayed for years and years.

At last, after about twenty years in Cathay, they decided to return to their home. Kublai Khan did not want them to go, but finally allowed them to return to their own people.

When they arrived in Venice, no one knew them. They had been away so long they had almost forgotten how to speak their own language, and they talked like foreigners. Their clothes were different from those worn by the people in Venice and they had become ragged from their long trip. No one could believe that these ragged, dirty strangers were the same fine gentlemen who had left Venice almost twenty years before.

The Polos told their townspeople all about their adventures and the wonderfully rich lands and cities that they had visited. But the people only laughed at them.

Then the Polos ripped open their ragged garments, and out fell magnificent and costly jewels—diamonds, rubies,

sapphires, and pearls—enough to buy a kingdom. The people looked in wonder and amazement, and began to believe them.

Marco Polo later was caught in a fight that was going on between cities, and he was thrown into prison. While he was there, he told his stories to a man who wrote them down. These writings were put into a book called *The Travels of Marco Polo.* You can read this book today, although we can't believe all the tales. We know Marco Polo exaggerated a great many things because he wanted to tell an amazing story. But he told also of the many real achievements of the people of the East—their beautiful art and literature, and their discovery and use of gunpowder, cannon, and the compass.

above left: Marco Polo watches a Chinese dragon-dance

below left: Map showing Marco Polo's journeys to the East

above: Portrait of Marco Polo

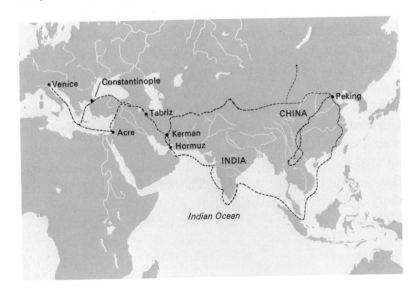

Rise of the Monarchies

By the fourteenth century, both England and France were becoming strong. Their kings were running a government bound by customs and laws. They both were national monarchies. In England the feudal lords had a say in government because of the Magna Carta and other customs. Law had been further developed and there was now a single legal system.

In France the situation was similar but significantly different. The French king had no Magna Carta. Although he had absolute power over his royal land, he did not have much authority over the lands or territory of his lords. France had a group like a parliament. It was called the Estates General. But unlike the English Parliament they had no real power. They couldn't make the king agree to things as the English had done. The king didn't need them to vote for taxes, so he called their help only when he wanted it.

Generally, feudalism was weaker in Europe. The people felt they belonged together despite their differences. The invasions had stopped. People had intermarried and they belonged to the same church. The feeling of nationalism grew in many areas, but particularly in England and France. England had a wood industry and this brought her money. France had had peace for nearly a hundred years. The population increased. Trade and industry grew.

Peace and happiness reigned—until both countries were ruined by a war that was fought off and on for over one hundred years.

England and France battled for land from 1337 to 1453. England still had some land in France that King John hadn't lost—Gascony and Guienne (ghee-ehn'). France wanted this land and England didn't want to give it up. But this didn't start the war. The war started because the king of England, Edward III, wanted to be made king of France.

Edward III's mother was the daughter of the former King Philip the Fair. Because he was a nephew of the former king of France, Edward III said he had a right to rule France. French nobles disagreed and picked another nephew of Philip who took the name Philip IV. So Edward started a war to take France, and the war he started lasted more than a hundred years. This is known as the *Hundred Years' War*.

The first period of the war lasted forty-three years— from 1337 to 1380. It started with the English invasion of France. The first great battle was fought at a little place called Crécy (kray-see′). The English army was on foot and was made up chiefly of freemen led by nobles. Most members of the French army were knights clad in armor on horseback—and society people, most of whom were lords.

The French knights thought themselves much finer than the common English soldiers. But they were proved wrong.

The English soldiers used a new weapon called the *longbow*. This bow was over six feet long and arrows used were a yard long. This weapon shot arrows with terrific force, enough to pierce a knight's armor. So the English completely surprised and whipped the French knights.

above: French knights fight against the English longbows in the Battle of Crécy

117

Cannon were used by the English for the first time in this battle. The cannon, however, didn't do very much harm. The English simply tossed cannonballs at the enemy as one might throw a basketball or a football. This frightened the horses of the French but did little other damage. But this was the beginning of the end of knights and armor and feudalism.

In 1348, a terrible bubonic plague came from Asia. This deadly, contagious disease attacked Europe. It was much worse than the plagues in Athens or Rome had been, for this plague did not hit just one city or country. It spread far and wide over the land and killed more human beings than any war there had ever been. This plague was called *Black Death* because black spots appeared on the body of anyone who caught it, and he was certain to die within a few hours or days. No medicine had any effect.

The plague lasted two years and millions caught it. We think that at least one-third of the people in Europe died from it. Whole towns were wiped out.

The crops in the fields went to waste, for there was no one to gather them. Horses and cows roamed over the country at will. The plague attacked sailors at sea also and ships were found drifting about on the water with not a soul alive on board.

Some cannon were used by the English during the Battle of Crécy. The cannonballs were rocks wrapped in burlap that were blown out of the tubes when gunpowder was ignited

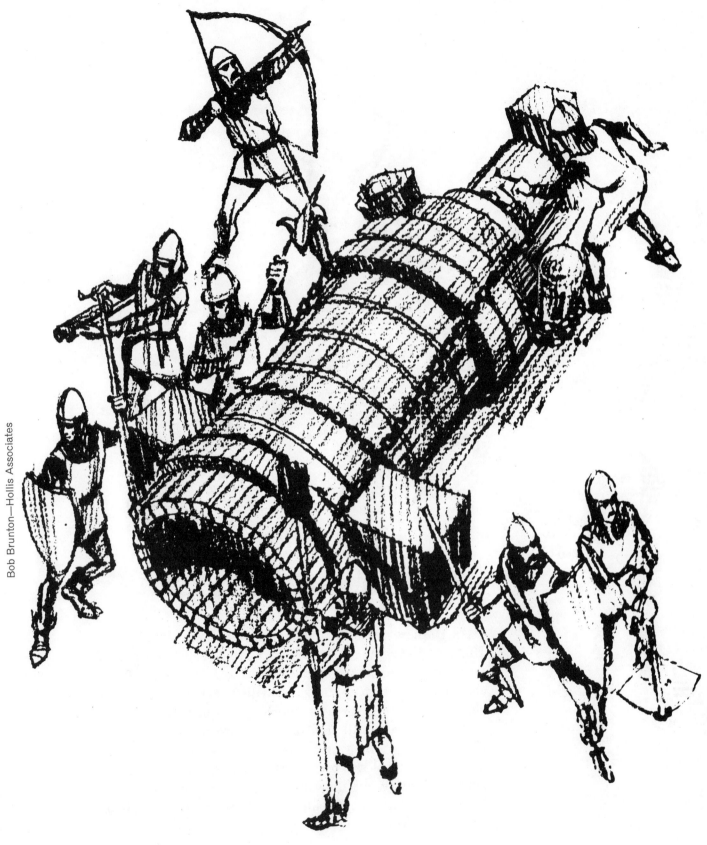

The heroine of the
French soliders,
Joan of Arc

As if there were not enough people dead already, the
Hundred Years' War went on year after year. The soldiers
who had fought at Crécy had been dead for years. Their
children had grown up, fought and died; so had their grand-
children and their great-grandchildren—and the English
and French were still fighting. The French prince at that
time was very young and weak. The French were almost
in despair—hopeless—because they had no strong leader to
help them drive out the English after all these years. It
looked as though they would have to submit to the rule of
an English king.

In a little French village at this time there was a poor peasant girl named Joan of Arc. As she watched her flocks of sheep, she heard "voices" calling to her. They told her she was the one who must lead the French armies, save France from England, and see the Dauphin crowned king of France in the cathedral of Reims. Joan went to the prince's nobles and told them of her visions. But they did not believe her story. They didn't think for a moment that a mere girl could do what hundreds of noble knights had failed to do.

To test her powers, however, they dressed up another man as the prince and put him on the throne while the prince stood at one side with the nobles. When Joan entered the royal hall, she took one look at the imposter pretending to be the prince, and without hesitating she walked past him. She went straight to the real prince. Kneeling before him she said, "I have come to lead your armies to victory." The prince gave her his flag and a suit of armor, and she rode out at the head of the French army. Joan was victorious at the battle of Orléans (ohr-lay-anh) and was hailed throughout the land as "Maid of Orléans." By July of 1429, the French soldiers took heart again. It seemed that the Lord had sent an angel to lead them, and they fought so hard and so bravely that they won many battles.

The English soldiers, however, thought that it was not the Lord but the devil who had sent Joan. She was not an angel but a witch, and they were afraid of her. During the battle at Compiègne (kohmp-yain') in May, 1430, she was betrayed and sold to her English enemies. The French king, whom she had served, didn't even try to save her, in spite of all she had done for him. Now that things were going his way, he didn't like to have a woman running things, and the soldiers didn't like to have a woman ordering them around. They were glad to get rid of her.

The English tried Joan of Arc for being a witch and found her guilty. They burned her alive at the stake on May 29, 1431.

Joan, however, seemed to have brought the French good luck. From that time on, France increased in strength, and after more than a hundred years of fighting, France at last drove the English out. By 1453, England had lost all her land in France except for Calais (kah-lay'). Neither side was really victorious, however, for the long and costly war left both sides weak. Years would pass before they were truly strong nations again.

Conclusion

The year 1453 has been used by historians to mark the end of the Medieval World. After the Hundred Years' War, the way men lived and the governments that ruled them were different. Feudalism and the powers of local lords gave way to the growth of national states ruled by strong kings and queens.

This year also saw the end of all that was left of the Roman Empire of the East. The city of Constantinople was again attacked by Moslems. They came from Turkey where they had already established an empire called Ottoman after a former king. Using modern methods of warfare—gunpowder and cannon—the Ottoman Turks broke through the city's walls and Constantinople became Turkish.

Many other things also happened during this time that gradually transformed the thinking and ways of the people. Perhaps the greatest new thing was discovered about 1440. This was the invention of moveable type which enabled the inventor, a German named Gutenberg, to print books cheaper and faster than had been possible previously. The first book he published was the book that was to the people of the time the most important in the world—the Bible. Now the Bible became available to hundreds. Gutenberg is called the father of printing because of his invention.

Books soon became popular. More people learned how to read. More reading meant more thinking and more learning, and education was increased. People began to learn about geography, history, and countless other things.

Other inventions put an end to the old and added to the beginning of the new. Gunpowder ended the usefulness of knights. Printing marked the end of mass ignorance. The compass put an end to the limiting of man's curiosity about unknown lands and seas. Entire new worlds and opportunities were discovered. Men began to advance learning and to explore, seeking new lands and new understanding of the earth, science, religion, and government. Man slowly but steadily, drawing on the experiences of the past, began developing a new and modern world.

The National States about 1453

INDEX: Young People's Story of the Medieval World

Type   *Century Expanded*
Typesetter   *American Typesetting Corporation*
Printer   *The Regensteiner Corporation*